What other law enforcement writers have to say about *Beyond Hope?*:

"Not only are the stories powerful, but the reader is drawn into all of the emotions experienced by an American law enforcement officer. Michael is a gifted writer who will make an impact on anyone who reads his work." –Lt. Randy Sutton, author of *A Cop's Life* and editor of *True Blue: Police Stories by Those Who Have Lived Them* and *True Blue II: To Protect and Serve.*

"*Beyond Hope?* offers a heart-wrenching look into the soul of a police officer immersed in the hopeless urban surroundings of a dying Midwestern city. The unforgiving streets of Saginaw, Michigan, are no place for the faint of heart. Author Michael East does not just open the door to this rabidly violent community- he shoves his readers through it. *Beyond Hope?* goes beyond simple portrayals of good guys and bad guys to give readers the most human and three-dimensional real-life cop stories available. This is simply an outstanding book!" – Peter Moskos, Professor of Law and Police Science at John Jay College of Criminal Justice, former Baltimore City Police Officer, and author of *Cop in the Hood: My Year Patrolling Baltimore's Eastern District.*

Devne

Beyond Hope?

One Cop's Fight for Survival in a Dying City

By Michael S. East

INFINITY
PUBLISHING.COM

Copyright © 2009 by Michael S. East

ISBN 0-7414-5337-1

Published by:

INFINITY
PUBLISHING.COM

*1094 New DeHaven Street, Suite 100
West Conshohocken, PA 19428-2713
Info@buybooksontheweb.com
www.buybooksontheweb.com
Toll-free (877) BUY BOOK
Local Phone (610) 941-9999
Fax (610) 941-9959*

Printed in the United States of America

Published July 2009

Dedication

This book is dedicated to my mother and father, and to the citizens of Saginaw, Michigan, a city I pray will eventually heal itself and realize its vast potential. As a man, as a writer and as a police officer, I remain a simple person who enjoys laughter, the love of family and the loyalty of good friends. Like most, I also strive to make my parents proud. Through my actions, my writing and my work I hope I am achieving this goal.

Table of Contents

Foreword 1

Knock, knock . . . 7

Mick 16

A Second Chance 20

Crime Takes No Holidays 27

Sunday Driver 35

Trick or Treat 44

"Frislee" 49

The Fall 53

First on Scene 62

Expect the Unexpected 67

Karen King 75

The Bungalow Motel 79

The Sentinel 86

Concrete Evidence 93

Cause for Celebration? 100

Calm Before the Storm 108

The Call   116

The Cop Attitude   125

Addictions   131

5:13 a.m.   136

Protect and Serve   141

A Good Day   148

Ride-A-Long   154

The Drive   163

Final Thoughts   166

Foreword

Let's get a couple things straight before we move on: As of this writing, I've never killed anybody, I've never shot anybody, and I've never been shot. These are the first three things most people ask when they learn that I'm a cop. I have, however, arrested uncountable felons and murderers, and I have looked into the lifeless, glazed-over eyes of the victims that have littered the streets of the urban shooting gallery where I work.

At least two publishers who took the time to review this project turned down *Beyond Hope?* because they felt it lacked a clear story arc. They were undoubtedly correct. The stories contained within these pages follow no logical pattern. Neither has my life as a cop. My transformation from naïve, enthusiastic rookie into disheartened and distrustful veteran was not a linear journey. This road of inner discovery has been an odd series of intertwining fears, revelations, accomplishments and failures. No one day is quite the same as the day which preceded it, but each new storyline has a personality all its own. *Beyond Hope?* purposely follows no set literary blueprint. To mold the events of my career into a pre-determined pattern would, I believe, be a disservice to those readers who want to experience the chaotic twists and turns which form the very essence of an urban cop's experiences.

Much of this book is dark and deeply depressing. The hatred in these urban streets is palpable, and the never-ending violence is suffocating and oppressive, but it is the true world in which most urban police officers toil for a day's wages. If this truth is not for you then turn back to the book store clerk before he gets the attention of the next customer in line and politely ask for a refund before it's too late. However, if you want to delve inside the heart, mind and soul of a cop charged with policing Saginaw, Michigan, a rabidly violent American city, I hope you enjoy this book.

Being a police officer is quite different than I imagined. I'm not quite sure when I got the itch to be a cop; I think it was somewhere in my mid-20s. Now that I wear a badge, I'm not sure why I continue to show up for work each day. Consciously, I tell myself the benefits package and the promised pension keep me tethered to this job. Subconsciously, I think I have an inner sense that my job simply is not yet complete. I'm not much for walking away from tasks left undone.

It was a gloriously beautiful spring afternoon in 1994 when I got the call from my background investigator at the Saginaw Police Department telling me I was hired. The subsequent years have been anything but glorious.

In that moment on the day when I was asked to join the police fraternity, my life changed completely. Within a five-day span, I quit my corporate suit-and-tie job, turned in my company car, packed up my life's belongings and exchanged my lakefront apartment in suburban Ann Arbor, Michigan, for a cramped one-bedroom place in what might best be described as an urban jungle. Looking back, these physical changes pale when compared to the psychological and philosophical changes that now make up my life's experience.

Prior to that spring the only dead bodies I had seen were nestled neatly within coffins inside funeral homes and churches, the work of the undertaker having polished the sharp edges of death. Raw and unpolished is the face of death when you're a cop. The Reaper comes quickly and violently in America's urban streets, and he doesn't clean up after himself.

Saginaw itself borders on the surreal. Located nearly two hours north of Detroit, it has suffered the same fate as many Midwestern industrial cities which made the mistake of putting all their economic eggs into one basket. As the 1800s turned into the 1900s, Saginaw's economy switched from being lumber industry driven to relying almost solely upon the auto industry. There was no safety net, and when the bottom fell out, it fell hard.

In 1970, Saginaw was a bustling industrial town of about 100,000 residents. But the city's economic fortunes were as fragile as a house of cards. And when one of the base cards – the auto industry – was pulled from the mix, all the others perched upon it went tumbling down.

Since 1970, the city of Saginaw has lost an average of about 1,000 residents per year, every year, and the population continues to wither. As people left in droves, businesses closed, jobs dried up and uncountable houses, which had lost their value, either sat vacant or were turned into rental units, many of which serve no purpose now other than housing the city's growing number of welfare-dependant addicts.

As the people left, Saginaw also became poorer. The often government-dependant economic lower class, which was much less affected by the spiraling local economy, largely stayed put. In the end, the hard-working backbone of Saginaw is what fled for more prosperous locales. Saginaw now is faced with the daunting task of staying fiscally solvent with a rapidly shrinking middle class.

The year I was hired the Saginaw Police Department had an authorized officer compliment of 165 cops. In 2000, when the dwindling tax base and sluggish economy combined to throw Saginaw into budgetary chaos, the police department began a trend of layoffs and cutbacks that has sliced it to a current count of 97 sworn officers – a nearly 41% decrease in manpower.

That 41% decrease, however, does not mirror the city's crime rate. During the years of public safety cutbacks, some justified the layoffs of police officers by saying the city was serving a smaller populace. While this may be true, it's not how many people, but *which* people we serve that has

3

caused the problem. As the middle class – those with jobs, property and a general sense of civility – fled, the people left behind were the poor, the under-educated and the unemployed. Oftentimes those who call the police are themselves at least half of the problem.

It's a vicious and seemingly endless cycle: A city's tax base shrinks, therefore services, such as public safety, must be cut back. But as police services decrease, crime rises and more taxpayers, tired of increasing crime, lose hope and move away. Sometimes taxes are levied to keep services at even marginally satisfactory levels. But this also alienates the middle class, which is burdened by paying more taxes for police services which it uses much less often than the poor, who pay virtually no taxes at all. The cycle is frightening to witness, and even more frightening to be a part of.

I'm not sure how many people have been murdered here since I pulled on my uniform for the first time, but I know it numbers in the hundreds. In 2006 alone, this city of about 57,000 residents - I have taken an oath to protect and serve them – suffered through the carnage of 140 shootings and 26 homicides. That does not include the hundreds of shootouts and drive-bys where the bullets missed their marks.

The prior year had been relatively slow, murder-wise, with only 17 people shoved through death's door. Saginaw often has an annual per capita violent crime rate higher than more recognizable cities like New York, Los Angeles and Chicago, and its per capita murder rate is equally unsettling. The community I serve has found a way to combine big city crime with a smaller town feel. And the crime, it seems, never ends.

Being a police officer in Saginaw is a sort of organized chaos, knowing what to do through sheer repetition despite the urgent, disorderly appearance of it all. The job presents an odd paradox: There's an unbelievable rush in knowing you can deal with the evil . . . and an unfathomable darkness in knowing you have to. The highs are very high and the lows can make you questions your life's very purpose. There are car chases, foot chases, armed standoffs and endless brushes with death. Police resources are slim, but when you have little to work with you learn how to get by.

Somehow I managed to survive my rookie years, when it was all about the gun and the badge and the perceived power they bring. That bravado has since given way to common sense, and now my thoughts center around survival. Ninety-seven cops don't own Saginaw's streets - those streets are the property of the thousands of thieves, dope-dealers, gang-bangers and murderers that populate this city. I find myself now just an average cop in not-so-average surroundings. I have saved a few lives and earned a few awards, and I have been fortunate enough not to have been killed yet. I have seen much, but I am a long way from knowing it all.

But some things I *do* know. I have been a cop for 15 years, but it feels like a lifetime. I shed tears over the horrible murder of Karen King and my inability to help her. I was sickened by the case of a Saginaw teen that was murdered, sliced open and dumped in the woods, his body systematically turned over by his murderer so the wildlife might eat his carcass and destroy the evidence. I have grown weary of seeing mothers scream in horror at the sight of their sons lying limp and lifeless in the streets. And I will never, ever, look at death the same again. *These things* I know for sure.

A few years ago, during a radio interview regarding another book I had written, the interviewer insinuated that my views of Saginaw are slanted toward negativity. He was undoubtedly correct.

As he pointed out, there are some positive things happening in Saginaw, Michigan. Saginaw County residents a few years ago agreed to shoulder a tax for the county to purchase and renovate what is now the Dow Event Center. This venue draws hundreds of thousands of people to downtown Saginaw annually for its shows, concerts and the Saginaw Spirit junior hockey team. Likewise, places like the recently renovated Temple Theatre, the Saginaw Children's Zoo, The Montague Inn and the downtown Castle Museum provide wonderful destinations and entertainment for people living in and around the area.

The recent re-development of Saginaw's riverfront with newly built medical offices has provided a beacon of hope and a new direction – medical technology – for the city's economic revitalization. To discount these positive strides and the people who have made them possible would be a disservice to the citizens of my adopted hometown.

There are many fine people working hard to help save the city I serve. But off the beaten path, away from the crowds and the lights and the noise of Saginaw's re-development, lie the dark streets and the murderous minds that make this one hell of a dangerous city. These are the places where my days are spent and my views are formed. *Beyond Hope?* contains some of my experiences as a Saginaw police officer. As in real life, a very rare few of them are positive.

The elusive uplifting moments still exist: a smile from a child, the soft touch of an elderly person's handshake, or a sincere talk with a homeless man or a prostitute, people that I sometimes realize are far more normal than they appear. These are the small moral victories that fuel my survival. I often have to dig deep to find them.

Through the good times and the bad there has been an underlying feeling of hopelessness about my career as a cop. Retirement awaits me now several years in the future. God willing, on some not-too-distant day, I will turn in my sidearm, put my badge into a box, and tuck it away in some forgotten place, a place I hope my nightmares might also find silent storage. But there is much work to do before that day and I do not want to leave my task undone.

For now, I will continue to chase the dream of peace that I hope to find in retirement. For now, I will try to stay one step ahead of the death and violence that surround me. I'm just not sure if that will be possible.

Knock, knock...

The pounding on my hotel room door forces me awake with the kind of jolt you get from jumping into a cold lake on a September day. It is the distinct, angry, fist-slamming type of pounding that can signal only trouble.

"Open that door, motherfucker! Open that door, man; we know you're in there!"

The men beating on my hotel room door are black and sound like they are in their 20's or 30's. And they are pissed off about something.

Rolling out of bed and on to the floor away from the door, it doesn't take long to realize I am in a world of trouble. But why? I have been in town for less than 12 hours and have talked to only the hotel desk clerk and the drive-thru girl at *Arby's*. I haven't had time to make enemies.

In five hours I am scheduled to sit before an inter-view panel at the Saginaw Police Department and explain why they should hire me. Will I even live that long? Do the guys pounding on the other side of this door know I'm a wannabe cop? I have heard many unpleasant things about Saginaw, Michigan, but good God, do they hate the police so much here that they hunt down applicants when they come to town for an interview?

It is now 3:10 a.m. on a Monday. To this point my day had been strange yet uneventful. I arrived in Buena Vista Township, a suburb which borders Saginaw to the east and south, at about 2 p.m. on a frigid November Sunday, and checked into this hotel, an established national chain which is clearly not profitable at this location, but is still clean enough to be a decent deal at $59 a night.

On a way-past-its-prime hotel television I had watched the Detroit Lions lose to the Green Bay Packers in the usual bumbling manner in which I had become accustomed to watching Detroit's version of pro football over the years. The steady hum of traffic on nearby Interstate 75 teamed up with a ho-hum football game to mentally wear me down through most of the afternoon. I was ready for a nap by four-thirty, but it was far too early for sleep. With few options for passing the time, I pulled on a worn pair of tennis shoes and set out for a lengthy jog to clear my head and prepare for Monday's interview.

My hotel room door opened directly into the parking lot on the east side of the building, and as the first rush of cold winter air struck my face, I was snapped awake in an instant. The sky was a deep blue, and an icy wind whipped through the air the inch of old snow that had been deposited the night before, stinging my eyes and face as I started off on a slow pace.

The hotel where I am lodged is of average size, boasting about 80 rooms, and a restaurant and lounge, which are housed in a separate building. Fewer than 10 cars scattered the parking lot, however. This is not the type of travel stopover people plan on purpose. It is, rather, a place where overt drunkenness, an overwhelming need for sleep, or an extramarital affair likely accounts for the majority of business.

I made my way toward the street and looked south where another chain hotel consumed a corner lot equal in size to my hotel. The accommodations there didn't appear much better than what I was currently experiencing. Like my hotel, it appeared to be the kind of place that changes names every few years.

Traffic was light and I turned north and jogged past several gas stations and convenience stores. Across the street was the Fort-Saginaw Mall, a place, I immediately thought, that was a mall in name only. Beyond a huge, nearly empty parking lot, a behemoth of a building stretched the length of several city blocks. It did not boast the glass, bright colors and linear attractiveness of more modern shopping centers; far from it. This building oozed depression. Long since void of big-named retailers, the cement-gray exterior meshed well with the local landscape. Damaged shopping carts littered the parking lot. A more deeply damaged community lay beyond.

Within moments the mall was out of sight and the scenery turned more residential, yet no less depressing. The shoebox type houses I passed could be described as modest at best. There were no sidewalks and the narrow roads made for nervous moments when cars passed. Most lawns and driveways were cluttered with junk, or cars somewhere in the process of being repaired, the speed of these repairs being given no apparent priority.

As I crept along the narrow streets, I became keenly aware that I was being watched. Then the realization struck me that I had not seen another white person since leaving behind the busy intersection near my hotel. Curtains moved at some houses as I passed, although I could not distinguish the persons behind the shrouds. At one house, a young black child stared incredulously as I jogged down his street. After a moment he broke his gaze to run inside and retrieve an adult, who joined him in silent shock as a white man passed through their neighborhood.

I had jogged only a couple miles, but felt like I had traveled much further, in terms of both time and distance. My return trip back to the hotel was every bit as eye-opening, yet uneventful, punctuated only by my one close encounter with another white person.

I saw the blue-and-white Buena Vista Township police cruiser approaching from a couple blocks away. The car drew closer and I could see the officer inside was a white man in his late 30's with unkempt hair and a mustache. He stared at me with an expression that I remember to this day, an expression that, put into words, clearly said: *What the fuck is your white ass doing jogging in this neighborhood?* We passed in one of those slow-motion gazes that lasts mere seconds yet remains for a lifetime. That is the first time I consciously thought to ask myself: *What the hell am I doing in this place?* I have re-visited that question hundreds of times since.

"Motherfucker, I said open up!"

The pounding at my hotel room door has resumed. *Now what?* The nightstand, and the phone perched upon it, is on the other side of the bed, closest to the door, which I am sure is going to burst open at any moment. Even if I get to the phone I am sure the cops aren't going to get here in time to help. I have no weapons, no means to defend myself. Looking around the room in a semi-panic I realize one thing quickly – I am fucked.

Then silence.

The pounding stops and the voices become muffled. I make my way quietly toward the door, simultaneously listening while striving to maintain my own silence. I can make out half drunken whispers from the other side of the door.

"Naw, this is the wrong room."

"You sure?"

"Shit, I just remembered, he's on the second floor, man."

"You dumb motherfucker."

With that exchange the men make their way around the corner of the building toward the stairwell.

After calling the front desk clerk to report the incident, with hopes she will contact the police, I double-check my door locks and slink back into bed for what will surely be a sleepless rest of the night. My eyes do not close again.

A few hours later, a cold, blustery morning waits as I climb into my white Chevy Beretta for the 10-minute drive to the Saginaw Police Department, which sits on the south end of what used to be a prosperous, vibrant downtown. Low, rolling gray November clouds provides the canvas for a disheartening portrait of a terminally ill city.

Block after block I forge ahead, slowing to take in the sights, the tell-tale signs of a metropolis in demise: a boarded up fast food chicken joint, re-sale shops, a pawn broker, and vacant filling stations, their islands stripped of gas pumps, their broken windows exposing places where workers used to toil for a day's wage. Some blocks are void of anything, save an abandoned house or two, the 3,500-square-foot, three-story style that used to provide shelter for the larger families more common in days long since past, structures in such a rotted state, my imagination cannot begin to see prosperity having ever resided there. Nearby, driveways sprout from the road and lead into nowhere, tapering off into grassy, weed-covered abysses - grave markers of sorts for structures which have already met their demise.

Up ahead, a larger building dominates the skyline, its 11 floors rising high above nearby buildings. The structure is brick, and one wall is marked with an aged advertisement, the paint faded to the extent I cannot discern what product it used to beckon to passersby. Closer inspection reveals this building, too, is abandoned, its windows broken, its bricks slowly loosening. Part of the sidewalk beneath the tattered edifice is closed to the public. Fallen, broken bricks and shards of glass litter the nearby sidewalk.

Looking around I see that other buildings have met a similar fate. Street after street, structures of various sizes, shapes and histories are deserted, their rusted security gates permanently closed, garbage swirling around inside. Scattered here and there are outposts of liveliness: A United States federal office building, a State of Michigan office building, three or four banks, and several small businesses, which appear to be holding on for dear life.

Oddly enough, early morning traffic is fairly heavy. Traffic lights keep time and order at intersections that, I now realize, seem much too busy for this place. *Where are all these people going? What do they do here?* The only people not in cars are people I imagine to be either street bums or prostitutes, although I have had very little experience with either during what I just now realize has been a somewhat sheltered life.

I keep thinking of those old cowboy movies and gangster films, the ones where the shootouts take place in an old western town or an inner city streetscape, constructed on some dusty back lot of a Hollywood studio. The feel here is the same: there are buildings, lots of buildings, buildings here and buildings there, but there is nothing behind them, save for the ghosts of yesteryear. Downtown Saginaw strikes me as little more than one very large facade.

I had seen similar scenes before, driving through areas of Detroit. But those sights were always seen at faster speeds on the way to take in a Detroit Tigers or Detroit Red Wings game. The depressing landscape of The Motor City always seemed less personal and was tempered with ultimately spending several hours in a vibrant, crowded ballpark or hockey arena, the history of its sports teams and big-league feel assuring me that the city of Detroit is here to stay.

Saginaw's long-term survival, I think, is not so assured.

I have never been to Saginaw, Michigan, prior to this day, although I had studied its history for the sake of my upcoming interview. For instance, I knew Saginaw had claimed nearly 100,000 residents as recently as 1970, but that number had shrunk to about 69,000 by the early 1990's. I knew the automotive industry had been both a boon and a curse to this place. And I knew crime was running rampant, although I had no way of knowing how that would affect my life in years to come.

Regardless of what I knew, or thought I knew, this morning's sights leave me with one unshakeable thought – Saginaw, Michigan looks like a city that could simply cease to exist at any given point in time, fading into memory the way the souls in these empty buildings had done. For the second time I wonder what I am doing here, looking for a future in a city that itself appears to have none.

I suddenly snap back to reality and realize three blocks too late that I passed the police department. I think briefly about just continuing on, putting behind me any thoughts of working in such a place. The deliberation, however, is brief and I decide at the very least I can use the interviewing experience. It is 1993, the current job market for cops is lousy, and my employment prospects in the field of law enforcement are quickly dwindling. I had tested and interviewed in other municipalities in Michigan and Ohio and had come up empty. At one cattle call in Toledo, Ohio, there were more than 2,000 applicants for about 20 jobs. I knew if I ever wanted to become a cop, I may very well have to start in a place like Saginaw simply to gain enough experience to make myself more marketable.

The interior of the Saginaw Police Department is every bit as drab as I expect. The dull red bricks and dimly lit lobby do little to warm me from the cold wind outside. To my left, eight slightly crooked black-and-white photos of Saginaw police officers killed in the line of duty sit above a glass display case which houses some dusty police memorabilia. To my right, a bum slumbers quietly on a bench, his life's collection of belongings sitting in two plastic bags on the floor. Directly ahead, a sober-faced desk officer directs me up the stairs without a hint of sociability.

On the second floor I am greeted in a friendlier manner by a secretary, and after declining an offer for coffee, I sit silently with two strangers – competitors for the same cop jobs – as I wait for my turn to interview. The two guys sitting near me both appear to be recent college graduates. Conversely, at 28, I am a little late trying to start my career as a cop, but I hold out hope that somebody somewhere will be impressed with my work history and life experience. I silently wonder if these guys are as unimpressed with Saginaw as I am, but I dare not pose that question aloud. For now the three of us sit in silence, occasionally catching one another's eyes in fleeting glimpses as we size up the competition.

Twenty minutes later I am led into a large conference room for my interview with a panel of three persons – a sergeant, a deputy chief and a civilian from Saginaw's Employee Services Department. The room is large enough, but an over-sized conference table gives it a cramped feel. Still, the interview itself is friendlier than most I have been through, and I feel relaxed from the start. Having experienced last night's turmoil, not getting hired here is not the worst thing that can happen to me. As expected, many of the standard situational questions revolve around racial issues with an underlying emphasis on honesty and integrity. My answers come quick and sincere and I immediately feel my confidence building. Hell, less than six hours ago I thought I was going to be robbed or killed by thugs in a dumpy hotel room. What could these people throw at me that is any worse?

The end of the interview comes about half an hour after the start, and the deputy chief asks if I have anything else to add. My final sales pitch revolves around education and communication skills. With college degrees in journalism and public relations, my written and oral communication skills are top-notch, I proclaim. I close with the following statement: "I don't know much about being a police officer yet, but I am a great communicator, and I would much rather talk my way out of a fight than get into one."

That simple final statement brings silent nods of agreement from two of the three sitting in judgment of my qualifications, and earns a broad smile from the deputy chief. However, we part with the sort of lame handshakes that are given by people worn down by weeks of fake smiles and pseudo courteousness. But the deputy chief, as he escorts me from the room, offers a wink and a smile and whispers: "Keep working on those communication skills."

My balloon of confidence deflates with that statement as I walk down a hallway to let the secretary know I am leaving. Was he mocking me? My parting pitch, my ace in the hole, was a flop, lost in the mix of hundreds of other pitches given by hundred of other applicants! *Keep working on those communication skills?* What the hell is that supposed to mean? I've been sharpening these skills for 10 years. That was supposed to be my edge, the difference between me and the next guy.

The secretary is as courteous upon my departure as she had been when I arrived. As I grab my overcoat from a nearby coat rack she informs me there had been about 1,700 applicants for the 26 available jobs. Of those, 600 or so are being interviewed. They will get back with me in a few weeks if they are interested.

My exit is quick and uneventful. I say nothing to the disgruntled desk officer, and don't pause at the photos of the eight dead cops on the wall. My departure goes unnoticed by the sleeping bum as well. Once outside, I think to myself that I will never see this place again, a thought that, at that particular moment, is not the least bit unsettling.

And as I drive away from Saginaw, Michigan for the first time, I have no idea of the life-changing events I will experience in this place.

Mick

It is 3:30 in the morning. A seven-year-old boy wakes to the sound of another beating, not unlike the ones he heard last night, last week and last month. He shakes off his grogginess as furniture and insults are hurled around in the dining room of the small, three-bedroom house he calls home. A single door separates him from the mayhem.

The house where the boy lives is the shoddiest on the block and its 900 square feet make for close living quarters. Numerous layers of paint over the years have rendered his bedroom door unable to close, and harsh words rush, unfiltered, through the gap between the door and its frame. The layers of the child's emotional scars run much deeper. Still, he walks silently behind the door, sits Indian-style on the worn carpet, listens, and tries to make sense of the madness that has haunted him for years.

They call him Mick, although that's not really his name; it's just a moniker attached to him by the man of the house; by the man who is right now beating his mother into submission. I've met many kids like Mick during my years on the streets. There are far more Micks in the world than there should be.

Mick is not sure where his nickname even came from. It pays homage to nobody in his family, nor to anyone that he has ever met. Eventually, he decided it was just a convenient way to circumvent his real name, lopping off a syllable and making it easier to be beckoned. Most kids' family nicknames are rooted in love or humor. Mick's is derived from neither. There is little love and even less humor in this house. He hates this name. He hates this house. He hates this life.

It has been years since I thought of Mick. But he has always been there, I guess, residing deep in my mind, lurking in the shadows just beyond conscious thought, alongside hundreds of others kids I have tried to help during my cop career. My memories of Mick, I think now, have served me well during my years on the streets. Sad as his story is, Mick has allowed me insights into things and people I might otherwise not understand. I owe that understanding to this young, suffering child.

Mick eventually tries to not listen as the fighting continues, unabated, for 20 minutes . . . 30 minutes . . . forever, it seems. He considers for a fleeting moment calling the police, but the phone, mounted on the kitchen wall two rooms and 20 feet away, is unreachable. He would have to cross the battlefield to get there, and that task would prove impossible. Besides, calling the police has proven fruitless in the past. The cops that had been to Mick's house before had done little more than give orders to "keep the noise down," a strong suggestion which was obeyed only until the police cruiser had rounded the corner of the block and vanished into the night.

The steady skin-on-skin smack of repeated slaps and punches echoes through the house and Mick knows his mother, as usual, is getting the worst of this bout. He stiffens as she tries in vein to fight back, but her blows are only verbal and they offer little defense.

Daybreak will bring a fresh set of battle scars and some heavily applied makeup. Mick has heard his mother explain away the bruises to inquiring neighbors many times. The explanations are always lame, told with such a lack of conviction that it is obvious she is trying to cover up an abusive relationship. Not that the explanations matter much. The neighbors who ask are simply gathering fodder for backyard, clothesline talk rather than providing a source of comfort for Mick's mother. Even at his age, Mick is not as innocent and unaware as most seven-year-old boys. He sees the way neighbors look at him. He sees the condescending way they treat his mother. But the worst of it is, he understands why. His family is, for the most part, the scourge of the neighborhood. His address is "the problem house on the block." That is something Mick just learned to live with.

It takes some time, but the pressures of Mick's home life eventually get to him. Unable to channel his frustrations, there are times when Mick literally beats his head against his bedroom wall, trying to knock the pain from his mind. The indentations he left in the plaster are far shallower than the holes the years have left in his heart.

Eventually, nights like these allow thoughts of suicide to gnaw at the fringes of his mind. The thoughts are fleeting, but they are there, making brief appearances, skittering like cockroaches you might see only when the lights first turn on. Mick's mind can concoct precious few alternatives to ending this suffering.

In the next room, the beating continues. Mick wishes he were man enough - or big enough - to stop the assault. He imagines himself charging into the next room to his mother's rescue and ending the violence. But he knows a scrawny seven-year-old has no chance of stopping this drunken rampage.

Mick's mind raises the suicide option again this night. He flips through the pros and cons, and reflects deeply on thoughts of the coldness, darkness and nothingness of taking one's own life. And while the nothingness seems a vast improvement to the *everythingness* which is his life, he puts the thoughts of his self-imposed demise on his mind's back burner. Mick slinks back into bed, clenches a pillow tightly over his head and holds on for another long ride. In his mind, he curses himself for being too small . . . too weak . . . too scared . . . to help. Eventually, he falls asleep, not knowing who, if anyone, will be there when he awakens. Muffled yelling and fighting are the last noises he hears before he quietly cries himself to sleep.

Many years have passed since the days of Mick's childhood. He was a troubled kid running the gamut of dysfunctional family life – abandonment, alcoholism, divorce, spouse abuse, and the shame only a child can feel when his schoolmates whisper that *his* family is "on the welfare." The encouragement and support one cop offered Mick fell woefully short of helping.

For my part, I was far too young to even know what words this child needed to hear. How can words ease the suffering of a child so young when the situation itself makes words useless? Words are just words. They don't stop the beatings. They don't stop the shame. They don't stop the pain.

The beating continued this night. The help that was so desperately needed never came. And Mick's hell continued . . . at least for a while.

A Second Chance

A bitter cold February evening years ago may have been the first time I realized the startling seriousness of police work. In a fraction of a second that took an eternity to pass, on a call so routine it nearly cost a life, I was confronted with the life-and-death reality of law enforcement. Nearly three full years after pinning on a badge for the first time and becoming a member of the Saginaw Police Department, I learned the split-second decisions made during the course of a cop's career can never be re-lived. It is a lesson I may never forget.

The night air is brutally cold and the frigid temperatures are accompanied by a full moon, which hangs quietly in the clear evening sky. My shift has been slow thus far and the graveyard silence of this night is a welcome relief from the normally hectic, call-after-call pace of the 3 p.m.-to-11p.m. patrol shift.

I had recently accepted a position as a Field Training Officer (FTO), a job which requires extensive training of new police recruits. Despite my relative inexperience, I quickly grabbed the FTO opportunity, prompted, quite honestly, by the extra income the position offered.

The recruit I am training on this night is Dennis Bunch, a short, stocky officer in his mid-twenties with thinning hair and a friendly demeanor. Dennis appears to me to look more like an accountant than a police officer. A couple years from now, Dennis will leave the Saginaw Police Department to accept a similar position in his hometown of Lansing, Michigan. Despite his pending departure, the events of this evening will forever provide a common thread between us.

Despite the night's relative calm, when we are dispatched to a residence on the city's east side, I let out a sigh of frustration at the stupidity of the call. Central Dispatch advises us that an elderly man has contacted them because he is concerned for the welfare of his grandson. The grandson had telephoned him earlier and said he was at a friend's house and some guys had come over and threatened the boy and his friends with guns. Apparently, nobody had been hurt, but the grandfather still wants us to check and see that his grandson is okay.

Because grandpa is unsure of the exact address from which his grandson called, we check several different residences, accompanied by another two-man training car that is dispatched as our backup. Each time we check a house, we are unable to locate the grandson. Eventually, as grandpa remembers another possible location and relays it to Central Dispatch, we are sent to yet another residence. It is at the fourth house that we finally locate the grandson.

Driving south through a neighborhood comprised of little more than shoebox-like houses and snow-covered abandoned cars, we pull up curbside, headlights extinguished, about 25 yards from a small white, one-story home. I recognize the house as one where I have been on prior occasions for gang-related activity. Several teenagers standing outside the front door of the residence, having spotted our police cars, immediately run inside the home, slamming the door behind them.

Unsure of what is happening, but keeping in mind the call involves weapons, Dennis and I quickly make our way through the foot-deep snow to the rear of the house, while the other FTO and his recruit officer approach the front door. We are at the rear of the house for no more than 15 seconds when the two officers on the other side of the residence beat on the front door and announce: "Police! Open the Door!"

Michael S. East

Immediately, the back door of the house creaks open. Light from the home's interior spills out and a large, cartoon-shaped likeness of a doorway is cast into the snowy yard. When a teenage boy walks out of the door onto a small cement-slab porch, the first thing I see is the black handgun clutched in his right hand, which he quickly turns toward me. This is my worst nightmare. By the time my mind yells the word *Gun!* – exclamation point included - I am staring at the business end of what appears to be a 9mm handgun, not much different from the one I am now swinging from my side toward the kid in an attempt to get off the first shot. *Shoot him! Shoot him!* My brain screams.

The teen is no more than seven feet away and, as I subconsciously await the muzzle flash from his gun and the excruciating pain that will surely follow, I simultaneously yell: "Drop the gun! Drop that fucking gun! Drop that fucking gun!" Unknowingly, I also seek cover, backing up two feet, partially hiding my body behind the corner of the house. It is during these split seconds, which pass like hours, that my mind registers the confusion on the boy's face.

While my brain is already screaming the question: *Why haven't you killed this kid yet?* it is also telling me - very clearly - that the kid is not going to shoot. My finger starts a trigger squeeze, but stops short of unleashing lead. *Why am I hesitating?* The kid's eyes are locked on mine. *Shoot him!* My finger stops. Reason stops. Time stops.

The unsteadiness in the kid's hand and the confusion in his eyes tell me the kid is simply not going to pull the trigger. He throws his gun to the ground now as if it is burning his hands. Holstering my own weapon as I reach for the kid and take him to the ground, I am soon joined by Dennis, who had sought cover behind a tree. He had also nearly shot the kid while repeating my commands. As we handcuff the teen, all I can manage is to repeatedly yell: "What the fuck are you thinking? What the fuck are you thinking?" His response comes as nothing more than a confused stare as we pull him, now handcuffed, from the snow.

22

As Dennis takes the teen to our patrol car, I retrieve the handgun that he had thrown into the snow near my feet. I am shocked and equally infuriated to find it is nothing more than a very realistic-looking pellet gun. *I almost killed a kid over a pellet gun!*

Heading to the patrol car, fake gun in hand, I open the back door to confront the teen face-to-face. But I am immediately struck with how innocent this kid now looks. Taking the gun out of the picture has changed his appearance dramatically.

"What the hell were you thinking, pointing a gun at the police?" I demand.

His reply comes low and sincere: "I didn't know you was the police. Some dudes had come over before and they had pulled some guns on us. I thought you was them."

"So you thought you would go after them with a pellet gun? Are you that stupid? You are lucky it was the police 'cause those motherfuckers would have blown your head off. I should have blown your head off. Do you realize you almost got killed tonight?"

In the same calm, sincere, what-do-you-mean tone of voice, he cocks his head like a dog responding to a high-pitched whistle and says simply: "No."

Eventually we lodge the teen at the Saginaw County Jail for felonious assault on a police officer. An hour or so of debriefing between Dennis and me follows with the discussion mainly involving the call and how it was handled. While Dennis receives nearly perfect scores for the day on my evaluation of how he handled the call, he has his own reasons for not shooting the gun-wielding teen.

"Shit, you're the FTO. I was just waiting to see what you would do. I was just trying to get my ass behind that tree," he replies when asked why he had not shot the kid. The nervousness in his laughter is apparent as we part ways at the end of the shift. As I walk alone now toward my car, the "what ifs" are still playing in my mind. *What if the gun had been real? What if the kid had shot? What if I had killed him? What if a cop does not respond to training in life-and-death situations the way he is supposed to?*

I drive home this night thanking God that I did not kill this kid, but angry as hell at myself for *not* killing him. I was supposed to – I was trained to – kill in this situation, and yet I did not. Why? Am I not willing to kill? Is my decision-making process too slow? Did I not kill him because of race? I am white, he is black, and Saginaw is one seriously racially divided community. Had I shot this kid, I know a racial firestorm would have ensued. Did I not take this kid's life because subconsciously I feared public perception? These thoughts swirl in my mind for hours, days, months . . . even to this very day.

The next morning I am awakened early by a telephone call from Jerry Schneider, the weekend duty detective, wanting to ask me about the previous night's events. I recognize Jerry as a guy of more than 20 years on the job and I know him by face and name only. Conversely, to Jerry I am undoubtedly just one of the 26 recruits who had been hired in May of 1994 – another faceless, nameless young cop with a lot of cop road left to travel.

"My main question is why didn't you kill this guy?" Jerry asks. *Here we go; here comes the criticism.* I silently rub my eyes and try to shake off my morning grogginess as I struggle to put an answer into words.

I scroll through my explanation of how I thought the gun was real and I spent a lifetime of seconds awaiting the pain from the first shot when I encountered the teen. However, I tell Jerry, I simply saw in the kid's eyes and the nervous way he held the gun that he was not going to pull the trigger. Jerry's response is more kind than I anticipate.

"Well, the only person who knows why you didn't shoot this kid is you. No matter what anybody says, you are the one who had to decide whether or not to shoot this kid. Don't listen to anyone else," Jerry responds, anticipating the second-guessing I will undoubtedly receive from co-workers. "With what I'm going to tell you I think you'll be glad you didn't shoot him. I just got back from interviewing the kid in jail. He is 17 years old and has never had a recorded contact with the police. He has never been a witness, a victim, a suspect or a reporter of a crime with our department. I also spoke to his mother and she tells me her son has the mentality of a middle-school kid. He still doesn't know why he's in trouble. I think you would have felt pretty bad if you had killed this kid. Don't beat yourself up over this. You did what you thought was the right thing to do."

Weeks pass and eventually I am subpoenaed to appear at a pre-trial hearing on the case. Jerry and I meet with the teen and his mother. A plea bargain has been worked out with the assistant prosecutor, but Jerry has refused to agree to the deal without my approval. He also wants me to meet the kid's mother before deciding on the plea arrangement.

Standing in the courthouse hallway, the woman immediately strikes me as a kind-looking person. Slight of build with tired eyes, she speaks appreciatively of the detective's work on her son's case. Her son, meanwhile, stands silently staring at the floor. We talk briefly and I agree to the plea bargain. The mother then thanks me, not for having shown the restraint to not have killed her son weeks earlier, but for agreeing to the deal which will keep him out of jail. With that she turns and walks away, her son staring at me in a manner which can best be described as confused. I have not seen him since.

Looking back on the events of that evening, it remains one of the proudest, yet most disappointing, days of my career. It was a day when all my training failed me miserably because I failed to take a young man's life. Had my instincts been wrong, my hesitation could have cost my own life, yet by the grace of God, everyone survived.

The day's incident appeared in no newspapers; it's only a good story, it would seem, when the cop kills the bad guy because then there's room for debate. I received no awards nor recognition for my actions that day, save for a verbal pat on the back from a detective who in his days has seen much worse, and who was now nearing the end of his own long career. My only other acknowledgement came in the form of locker room ridicule from a sergeant and a few co-workers, who told me I was wrong for *not* killing the teen.

So goes the life of a cop.

Oddly, it was on this particular night that I decided to start writing about the everyday experiences of police officers; of the highs and the lows, of the exciting and the mundane, of the lives we touch and of the lives we see lost. It is a job where hope and faith strike an odd balance with death and despair, and living to see retirement requires both physical and psychological resiliency.

It is a job I love, and a job I often love to hate.

Crime Takes No Holidays

I am exhausted - exhausted from the heat and humidity, exhausted from lack of sleep, exhausted from the weight of the violence of the day that ended for me a little more than 12 hours ago. It's nearly 6 p.m. on a sticky, hot and humid early July afternoon. My shift began three hours ago and my undershirt soaked through with sweat an hour after that.

Even by Saginaw standards, yesterday – the Fourth of July is always hectic for Saginaw's law enforcement community - was overwhelming. On a day meant to take notice of individual freedoms and celebrate various personal good fortunes, the streets of Saginaw ran red with blood. The SPD, and each individual officer, was stretched far beyond their respective limits as radio dispatchers spewed forth a call-after-call-after-call mix that included six shootings, one homicide and a flurry of drunken domestic assaults, gun calls, cuttings and home invasions which continued until nearly dawn, the night appropriately topped off with Michigan State Police troopers screaming for help at a large fight on the south end of the city as the clock approached 5 a.m.

As I drove home more than 15 hours after I had arrived for the previous day's work, the sun was starting to peek over the eastern skyline, outlining houses, finally quiet, where the night's revelers now lay in drunken hibernation. The air was thick with sulfur, a smell left behind by 12 hours of excessive neighborhood fireworks. Somewhere in the distance, relatives gathered at crime scenes and hospitals to mourn the dead and wounded from a night on the streets of a city with far too many uncivil civilians.

My eyes were half closed when I rolled slowly into my driveway. The shift's events faded when my head hit the pillow, and sleep came mercifully fast as my body and mind shut down after 15 hours of mayhem. Five hours later – a time frame that seemed to last mere minutes – my alarm clock signaled the start of a new day or, more accurately, a continuation of the shitty day I had seemingly just closed my eyes on.

A weary shower offered little motivation and I spent the next two pre-work hours catching up on household chores and reading the day's edition of the local newspaper, which tried to report, as if it were surprising, the violence I had seen firsthand. Even reporters have a hard time putting a new spin on murders in Saginaw, the act and the subsequent media coverage becoming somehow passé; Another day, another murder (yawn).

In the locker room as I dress and chat with co-workers about the hooliganism of the previous day, I silently pray for a quieter shift today. That prayer will go unanswered. My energy is tapped and I know I don't have the mental edge to be an effective cop today, an edge that when lost, greatly increases the risk to any cop's safety.

The first three hours of the shift are quiet, except for an encounter with a suicidal woman who had jammed a steak knife into her own belly. That relative calm now changes in an instant.

"Thirty-eight-T, are you going to be clearing soon?" a dispatcher bellows over the radio.

I am in my patrol car at the police station, getting ready to clear from my previous report call, and I know the other unit – "Thirty-eight" marking that unit's assigned patrol district and "T" marking it as a training unit with one experienced officer and a rookie in training – is at the station also. I also know that unit's assigned district encompasses an area near the police station, so whatever call had prompted the dispatcher to push 38-T to clear, it is going to be close by and it is going to be hot.

"Thirty-eight-T, we can clear. Go ahead," responds the not-very-confident voice of the recruit in training.

The dispatcher's words verify my assumptions about the call: "For Thirty-eight-T and any units to fill. Thirty-eight-T and any available units - South Warren and Emerson for a shooting. Caller states there is one black male teen shot, lying in the field at the corner."

"Thirty-eight-T, okay, from the 'The Walls'," the recruit responds.

The Saginaw Law Enforcement Operations Center had been built decades ago and its police parking lot is surrounded on one side by the building itself and on the other three sides by 14-foot-high walls which give the department the appearance of a fortress built to withstand an enemy invasion. The lot is accessed by any of four openings. Above each opening used to sit large, metal, roll-down doors, which could be sealed, presumably, if the department suddenly came under siege. During my first tour of the Saginaw Police Department, I remember thinking this place was built in case the riots of '67 ever happened again. Shortly after I hired on I found out the roll-down doors were no longer functional. In the late '90s the doors were removed from their perches altogether (I wish they would have been repaired). In any case, because of the physical layout of this area, officers routinely announce they are en route from "The Walls" when they respond to calls from the police station.

I break from "The Walls" within seconds, lights and siren announcing the urgency of my trip to the few prostitutes and vagrants who might take notice. "Thirty-seven, I'll be en route there also. Send me the call," I announce over the wail of my patrol car's siren.

"Thirty-seven, okay," responds the dispatcher.

The shooting scene is less than two dozen blocks from the police station and, with Thirty-eight-T riding in my wake, I feel confident with some luck and help from witnesses at the scene we might still catch the shooter close by.

When I roll onto the corner, there is nobody around. I start to think it is a prank call, until a middle-aged black couple behind a garage a few houses away points me to the west. There, about 100 feet into a vacant lot, a woman waves her arms. At her feet is a young black teen, lying face down in the grass.

The two officers from the other responding unit pull up behind me and the three of us reach the boy together. "He's still breathing!" the panicked woman screams.

The boy's white t-shirt has a blood stain about two inches in circumference near his left shoulder. He has another through-and-through wound to his arm. I am sure the first wound has probably pierced his heart. He lies perfectly still, with no signs of breaths being drawn, no moans of pain, no strain of a fight for survival.

Doug Stacer, the training officer next to me, known in this neighborhood simply as "glasses" for his bespectacled appearance, kneels down for a pulse. "Central, have the rig step it up!" I advise dispatch. Doug shakes his head ever so slightly to let me know that was a waste of breath. Like most cops, however, I try to err on the side of caution. I would rather let the medical people make the call when it comes to pronouncing the dead.

The next couple minutes are a blur of sirens, and screaming and running people. Each arriving officer takes up a post to push back the throng of onlookers who want to run up to the body. At scenes like this it seems everyone claims to somehow know, or be related to, the victim.

"We'll be starting a crime scene," I inform dispatch, more than anything to let a supervisor know their services will be needed, as well as those of the detective bureau. That announcement also starts in motion the act of the shift commander notifying the Chief and Deputy Chief that we are working an active homicide. The latter call is made mostly as a matter of courtesy. No high-ranking administrator wants to face the media about the city's latest victim of foul play without having knowledge of the event itself.

As I assist other officers taping off a crime scene, we each ask the dozens of on-lookers if they had seen the incident. This, more than anything, thins the crowd. Person after person answers with nothing more than a blank stare and a great view of their back as they shrug and walk away. This is the part of a crime scene that used to infuriate me, when people who later tell the media the police don't care, turn their collective backs on our questions. After a few years, however, my anger turned to apathy. I now find it impossible to help those who refuse to help themselves. I no longer can muster sympathy in exchange for silence.

Within 10 minutes of the shooting, an ambulance crew unceremoniously pronounces the victim dead, and the scene is swarming with detectives, officers and television news crews. More ominous, however, is the growing crowd of onlookers, which now numbers at least 150. Most stand on the other side of the thin yellow police tape. Others simply ignore the tape and walk into the scene. They are quickly grabbed and led out, drawing the ire of the crowd and prompting some anti-police shouts from those in attendance.

A new police recruit is left at the west end of the scene, nervously guarding the tape line where 75 or more people split their stares between him and the dead boy. Several teens storm away and grumble about "getting our guns and taking care of this." The recruit is unsettled, but hides it well.

A short time later the boy's mother wanders into the scene. I respond to her more softly than the other trespassers, mainly because this is a crucial point in the day. If she breaks out in a panic, screaming and crying, the energy of the crowd will quickly be directed against the police. I quietly whisper that she doesn't want to see her son like this. Another relative crosses the police line to help me. She walks the woman away. I thank her for her help with a silent, appreciative nod.

Scouring the scene we still have no witnesses, except for a couple people who heard the gunshots, but saw nothing.

Another television newsman arrives, walks up to the crime scene tape, ducks under it, and starts to walk toward a group of cops. He is quickly scolded and told to get his ass on the other side of the tape. The crowd seems to appreciate this. Sometimes the only people despised more than the police at homicide scenes are the news people trying to piece together a story for the nightly news.

After an hour or so a second ambulance arrives to transport the dead boy from the scene. I am relieved by this because the removal of the body always seems to calm the masses. My relief soon turns to anger, however, as a female paramedic waves me over to the ambulance.

"Could you do me a huge favor," she says.

I don't recognize her, but answer as politely as my tired and frazzled nerves allow. "Sure, what's up?"

"Will you help my partner pick up the body? If I have to do that, I swear to God, I'll freak," she asks, apparently oblivious to the fact that part of her job is dealing with dead people.

I am all at once amazed and disgusted. Over the years I have worked with many cops who don't want to pull their weight; cops who want to be called cops and carry a gun and flash a badge, but who do not under any circumstances want to get their hands dirty or be put in harm's way. She strikes me as the paramedic parallel of these types of officers. Her partner looks at me with a blank stare. I am sure he does not care for her much either.

"Fine," I reply, pulling on a pair of rubber gloves. My only concern is getting the body out of the scene to keep calm among the crowd. When another officer discovers what the paramedic asked, he takes a few verbal jabs at her. She responds in an all-too-cutesy voice: "I'm not kidding. I would *freak* if I had to do that!"

Now I can't resist. "Hey, you gotta do *me* a favor," I say rather blandly.

"Okay."

"There's a party store being robbed down the street. Will you take my gun and go handle it for me?"

Clearly not feeling the bite of my sarcasm, she laughs her cutesy laugh. "Sure," she giggles as she bats her eyes innocently at some other nearby cops. I turn now and start toward the dead child. I have neither the time nor the energy to make my point any clearer.

When I walk up, the dead teen has been turned onto his back for photos. The white sheet covering his face is transparent now thanks to a rain that has begun to fall. The wet sheet is now his death shroud, sticking to the high spots on his face - his cheeks, nose and forehead, leaving dark marks where his eyes and mouth are.

When we pull the sheet off, the boy's eyes are glazed and lifeless, and his now-stiff hands are clenched in fits of agony. His mouth is agape. I wonder if he knew he was dying when he finally dropped here. I wonder if his last thoughts were of hatred . . . or fear . . . or maybe, just maybe . . . remorse.

A detective halts us before we place the boy into the body bag. He removes a revolver from the boy's shorts pocket. The irony is thick and un-amusing. With that, the white bag is zipped shut, the body is slung onto a stretcher and another wasted life comes to an abrupt end.

Moments later, a new revelation comes to light. Detectives on the scene finally find someone to tell the truth and the truth is infuriating. Our original crime scene, constructed with what little information had been initially given to us, was not the real crime scene at all. The teen had actually been shot several houses to our west, where a large crowd had gathered, blocking the view of bullet casings and the teen's bicycle that now lay on the sidewalk. The entire time officers and medical personnel tended to the teen, formed a crime scene, asked neighbors and bystanders for information, and tried to ease the pain of relatives, evidence sat mere yards away. It appears people in the crowd knew all of the information about the shooting, including the identity of the shooter, but nobody stepped forward to help.

About a week prior to this incident, another young teen had been gunned down in the streets of an east side neighborhood in the early morning hours when streets in normal towns are void of inhabitants. Days later, the local newspaper ran an article in which the boy's relatives admonished police and city leaders for not closing down an after hours club the boy had attended the night of his death. The blame game was carried out paragraph after paragraph with the police department taking the brunt of the abuse. Predictably, not once in the article did the concerned relatives blame the anonymous shooter. Nor did they say why the child's family allowed him to freely roam the streets at a time when the only thing he could hope to find was trouble.

Later in the night, as I finish putting into report form my actions from the scene of another homicide, I think about the dozens of senseless murders I have seen over the years, and about the dead young men whose names I can no longer recall. For a brief moment I also ponder solutions to this problem of gangs and guns and youth violence. Then I think about the friends and families of many victims who shamelessly blame the police, of all people, for the murders of their children.

As I finish my report and press the "save" button, I shake my head and clear my mind. The solution to this problem is one I cannot even begin to fathom.

Sunday Driver

When I was growing up, my grandmother was a devout Catholic who was widowed at 49 and spent her remaining 34 years as a pillar of her church and her community. One of the many things she taught me is that Sunday is a day of rest. I have since learned there are no true days of rest when you're a cop.

It is a warm summer evening, but I am rejoicing in the fact a rare bit of luck has found its way to me - the air conditioner in my patrol car is working well today. As I creep slowly though an eastside neighborhood, I take extra caution at intersections. The summer grass has become so high on many uncut, vacant corner lots it renders me nearly blind to oncoming traffic. When warm weather hits for the season, the tall grass and crumbling houses give the appearance that the earth is trying to reclaim Saginaw, to pull it back down into the ground. Sometimes I think the thick waist-high grass and unchecked foliage will succeed. Maybe starting from scratch wouldn't be such a bad thing for this urban wasteland.

As I make my way to a mundane call, the details of which are too bland to expound upon, I hear Central Dispatch giving updates on a different call to three other cars. I don't recall any of the cars being given a priority run, so this call must have been sent to them via in-car computer. The fact that three cars are being sent also tips me off to the urgency of the matter to which they are attending. Normally, in-progress situations call for only two responding units. The only times Central Dispatch deviates from the playbook are when there is a shooting involved, or the call is of some other abnormally violent nature. My curiosity gets the best of me.

"Thirty-seven, I can divert to assist if you need another unit for that last call," I say into my radio mic. I am hoping for a positive response, but either way, I know I am heading for the hot call. Asking permission simply leaves me less vulnerable to a supervisor's scrutiny if things go to shit.

"Thirty-seven, I'll send you the call," a dispatcher replies, offering the response I want to hear.

When the nature of the run comes over my in-car computer, I know right away it will be a good one. The call is to assist the Detroit Police Department locating a possible homicide suspect. Apparently the suspect had fled Detroit earlier in the day with a vehicle that is equipped with a vehicle tracking system. The system, which can pinpoint a given auto's location, had tracked the suspect's late model SUV-style car to a neighborhood on Saginaw's east side.

I am near East Holland Avenue, a multi-lane main thoroughfare that dissects the city's east side, when I hear two other responding units call on checking the suspect's last known location. I am still several miles away, but close the gap quickly, breaking at red lights only long-enough to ensure the path is clear. Then Central Dispatch tosses in the inevitable monkey wrench that seems to find its way into most hot calls. "For responding units, the tracking system has gone down, and they've lost the signal."

I have just arrived in the area and my call-jumping efforts are now apparently wasted. Still, I check the surrounding blocks for the suspect, even though the lag time between the signal being lost and that detail being reported to us assuredly has given him a significant head start.

As luck would have it, it takes less than a minute for the original officer on scene to catch the break we need. "Forty-six, I've got a vehicle matching the suspect's car, pulling out of the Admiral gas station on East Holland."

"Forty-six has possible suspect vehicle, Admiral station on East Holland. All units stand by," the dispatcher reiterates.

I am close and find myself within view of the lead patrol car and a backup unit within seconds. My heart starts pumping hard now and I grip the steering wheel just a little tighter with the anticipation of some action. The next five minutes will be a mix of police academy driving school flashbacks and sheer adrenaline.

"Forty-six, we're going to get farther out on East Holland away from traffic before doing the stop," announces the lead officer. Ahead of him a black SUV-style vehicle eases its way eastbound in the southern most lane of traffic. As it creeps along, I can sense the apprehensiveness of the driver through the vehicle's movements. It is as if the vehicle itself is a living, breathing creature, reacting the same as prey being hunted in the wild. The car slows, and then speeds up, measuring the attentiveness of its stalkers. It moves side to side, seemingly trying to nudge cars away from its left side to ensure a path of escape. *This one isn't going down easy.*

I fall in behind the two other patrol units. Traffic has lightened somewhat, save for another car in front of the suspect and one on its left side.

"Forty-six, we're going to try the stop Holland east of Cumberland."

"Holland east of Cumberland," the dispatcher echoes. "All units stand by."

Simultaneously, the overhead lights of all three patrol cars come alive, and traffic comes to a near halt. The suspect vehicle creeps slowly side to side. Like a caged beast, the growl of the SUV's engine seems almost animalistic as it tries to clear a path of escape by intimidating the two civilian vehicles which have also pulled over.

The driver of the vehicle to the left of the suspect senses danger and his vehicle speeds off. However, its void is quickly filled by a patrol car, which forces the suspect back into his original lane. The car in front of the suspect rolls along slowly, trying to help contain our prey by not letting him through. "This is not good," I say aloud to myself. The suspect is getting wound up now and if he is armed, he might just open fire on Joe Good Citizen in front of him.

My fear for the safety of the anonymous citizen washes away quickly as the suspect makes his move. In an instant, the black SUV breaks free to the right and drives up onto a grassy embankment, leaving the roadway behind. *Here we go!*

"Forty-six, pursuit! He just left the roadway!" yells the lead officer.

I am sure Central Dispatch replies, but I have no recollection of radio traffic from this point on, only the unfiltered rush of pumping blood and the internal voice that I assume accompanies all officers during high-speed pursuits.

The black SUV darts along the grass for a hundred feet or so before jumping into the front parking lot of an *Arby's* restaurant, barely missing picnic tables where summertime diners often sit. I pull alongside him for a brief moment and I can see his face. It is the irrational face of panic and defiance. He stares back, looks right through me, swerves in my direction and then back the other way, jumping into another parking lot. The scene is complete mayhem for a moment as the three patrol cars try to hem in the maniac without crashing into each other. Finally, the SUV breaks free and accelerates eastbound onto East Holland Avenue.

The next major intersection is Outer Drive and I pray to God he turns here, although I know deep down he won't. He came here from Detroit and he's going to try to get back the same way, right down the busiest freeway in the state – Interstate-75 - which sits just a half mile away.

After running the stop light at Outer Drive and miraculously emerging unscathed, the suspect stomps the gas and gathers speed as he hits the on- ramp to southbound I-75. *This is not good; this is really not good.*

Had it been another time of year, I would have welcomed a wide open pursuit on this freeway. The clear path of the interstate drastically cuts down on the chances of the suspect ditching the car and engaging us in a foot pursuit. I hate foot pursuits, especially in the type of sweltering summer heat that is crushing down on the Saginaw Valley region today.

But the heat is not my concern now. This is Sunday. *Why does it have to be Sunday?* For Michganders, Sunday during the summer on southbound I-75 means only one thing – traffic . . . and lots of it. For as long as I can remember the weekend summertime ritual in Michigan is for tens of thousands of cottage owners to jump on I-75 north on Friday afternoon, exchanging the overcrowding of metropolitan Detroit for the perceived calm of the cottages and summer homes nestled around Northern Michigan's countless lakes and rivers.

Conversely, Sunday finds the droves of weekend travelers headed back southbound, their trailer-toting cars, SUVs, and oversized campers crowding the interstate, snarling traffic in stop-and-start bursts for miles on end. Punching my accelerator and looking ahead into the maze of metal laid out before me, disaster seems the only logical outcome.

When I hit the interstate, pedal to the floor, I immediately find myself – and the two patrol cars ahead of me, for that matter – at a distinct disadvantage. The suspect's late model SUV is built not only for looks, but it possesses two things our patrol vehicles lost years and countless miles ago – speed and dependable maneuverability.

When I started my career, the SPD had a new fleet of cars every couple years and two full-time mechanics to man the department's four-bay police garage. The air guns that used to keep pace with maintenance requests have long-since been silenced by budget cuts. The mechanics are gone, and the garage's silver double doors now remain closed.

I think back briefly now and remember when one of the first things I saw during my tour of the police station was the fleet of new Chevrolet Caprice police cars being readied for service, nestled in neat rows inside "The Walls."

"They've got Corvette engines. These babies can move," proclaimed our tour guide, an ill-tempered retired cop, who even now works in a civilian capacity with the department. And he was right. Those cars accelerated like rockets, literally pushing me back into the driver's seat when I went a bit too heavy on the gas pedal. *What I wouldn't give for one of those damn cars right now.*

But those were the cars of better days, the days when more cops, good equipment and even my keen sense of purpose were so common I took them for granted. The reality of this day finds me chasing a reported murder suspect in a car sporting well over 100,000 hard-driven miles with maintenance problems too lengthy to even consider.

The suspect's lead widens to about a quarter mile and the only thing keeping him that close is the heavy traffic. I can see some of the motorists panicking at the sight of the pursuit. Others are simply not paying attention, talking on cell phones and listening to the radio as potential disaster rushes up behind them at triple-digit speeds. These are the drivers who concern me the most.

I am able to push three lanes across to the far left lane through the smallest of openings, following a path the suspect had swathed seconds ago. Up ahead the two lead cars are struggling to keep pace as well. In my rearview mirror I can see the top lights of more patrol cars entering the freeway.

The suspect continues to jump lanes, nearly crashing a half dozen times. In an attempt to keep up, I jump onto the left shoulder, praying nobody abruptly pulls to their left and wrecks me. My patrol car shudders and coughs. I think briefly of a horse, which is about to lie down and die after being ridden too long in the desert. I coax my car aloud, trying to get it to perform just a little bit better, just a little bit longer: "C'mon, baby, you can do it. Keep up." The absurdity of my words brings a slight grin to my lips even as the pursuit pushes on.

The lead cars continue to shadow the suspect, weaving in and out of traffic in jerky, quickly conceived movements. The lane changes are so tight the scene reminds me of a real-life game of "Frogger." Tossing up a wake of trash and debris as I ride the left shoulder, I am still falling farther behind. I glance quickly at the speedometer. It reads slightly over 100 mph. There is little radio traffic as nobody wants to risk the distraction at these speeds. The only sounds I can hear are the faint sound of my siren in my subconscious and the pounding of my own heart, which apparently has found a new home next to my ears.

And then it happens.

The one thing that escapes the suspect – patience – prevents his escape this day. He holds the better hand. He has the better car. He was getting the best of us. But we held the bluff long enough and put on enough pressure that the suspect finally makes a mistake – a near fatal one at that.

Up ahead, I see the suspect panic and pull hard left in an attempt to find the clear path of the shoulder lane I now occupy less than a half mile behind him. But in his rush to escape, he overcompensates and slams into the cement barrier which separates northbound from southbound traffic. The impact causes a second overcompensation, this time to the right. The suspect's car shoots across three lanes of traffic and somehow misses the flow of swerving vehicles trying desperately to get out of the way.

No other cars are struck, but the suspect is not so lucky. After his out-of-control vehicle leaves the freeway, it travels down an embankment, hits a cement drainage tube, goes airborne and rolls four or five times, plowing through a fence and reaching the height of a treetop before crashing down right-side-up next to the same tree. The vehicle's windows and tires blow out and the engine is smoking when I screech to a halt at the side of the freeway and run toward the car.

The two lead officers are slightly ahead of me running toward the wreckage and, as I jump a large ditch which borders the freeway, I hear a distinct call for help.

"Hey, I'm stuck. Get me out of here!" When I look quizzically to the officer at my left, he is looking back and laughing slightly. Even in the midst of this chaotic car chase, I turn and look and I have to laugh as well. The officer who had piloted the second car in the chase, upon reaching the four-foot ditch next to the freeway, had opted to run through it rather than jump across. She stands there now, stuck knee-deep in mud, her Glock handgun pointed straight up in the air as she struggles to free herself.

The other officer and I stare for the briefest of seconds, share a chuckle, shrug our shoulders and leave her behind. She's not sinking any deeper, so she'll be okay there. There are more pressing issues up ahead where I am sure the suspect is dead.

We approach the suspect's wrecked car as tactically as possible and find him still alive, but trapped inside. It doesn't take long for a throng of officers, fire rescue and ambulances crews to descend upon the scene. The suspect is extracted from the carnage. He is dazed, but in amazingly good condition. He now has much bigger problems to answer to.

My mind compensates for my body's drop in adrenaline now as the chaos of my surroundings grinds into slow-motion mode for a moment. The sounds of the scene become muffled and I do a 360-degree turn and take it all in. As I look at the freeway traffic which is now at a standstill a hundred feet from the scene, all I can see are the stunned faces of motorists and passengers as they stare incredulously at the wreckage. My hearing returns to normal and in the distance I detect the buzz of grasshoppers in the air. I realize it has turned into quite a beautiful summer evening.

In the middle of the confusion, the previously trapped officer arrives at the suspect's car. She is muddied, she has a moderately bruised ego and she is minus one boot. She is slightly embarrassed, but virtually unharmed. She did her job well today. She's going home alive and with a good story to tell.

Isn't that all she can really hope for? I think to myself.

Isn't that all any of us can hope for?

Author's Note: Not long after this incident, the garage at the Saginaw Police Department was re-opened and a mechanic was hired to address the mounting concerns of many patrol officers regarding police vehicle safety. The grinding noise of air guns from the garage echoing off "The Walls" is a welcome sound as I depart the SPD each work day to deal with the more serious sounds of the real guns being put to use in the streets.

Trick or Treat

Although I cannot pinpoint the exact reason, I have always loved Halloween. Maybe the attraction is the same thing that drew me to law enforcement – that sense of uneasy anticipation you get when you know something dangerous can – and probably will – happen. The adrenaline rush of coming so close to death and things unknown is unmistakably raw, unmistakably pure.

There is one marked difference, however. The fear and perceived threat of Halloween night dissipates quickly when the sun rises on November 1st. On the streets there is no sigh of relief; the horror show begins anew with the start of each shift. For one distinct night in my life the reality of the streets and the commercialized macabre of the season intertwined to bring me on an unforgettable personal trip to death's doorstep.

It was several years ago and my perpetual love of Halloween had led me to request the night off. My lack of seniority, and the Saginaw Police Department's lack of available cops, however, brought back to my mailbox a Time-Off Request Form, adorned with a hand-written note from my shift commander, written in red ink: "Denied due to lack of manpower." So my mind was elsewhere as I trudged off sometime after 3 p.m. to start a work shift I wasn't very excited about. The events of the approaching night would re-focus my attention.

The late October air smells of decaying leaves and the streets are active with the buzz of children. I think about being at my own house, which is always decorated for Halloween sometimes before the leaves even change colors. To accent the décor, I dress in an all-black Grim Reaper costume – the irony of the disguise hadn't struck me when this tradition began – and silently hand out treats after emerging from the shadows. This process elicits a few startled screams from young children, and a few reserved handshakes or high fives from the less timid. Nearly everybody walks away content with the slight scare a stop at my doorstep offers.

As I shag a few non-descript calls for service, I anticipate the arrival of dusk and the costumes it will produce. In Saginaw most of the heavy trick-or-treating takes place on the city's west side, where kids get dropped off by the carload to roam the more prosperous neighborhoods in search of candy. My beat on the north east side of town is not the best place for costume observation, but it will have to suffice. Most families, it seems, regard walking the streets of Saginaw's east side as far too dangerous, Halloween or not. Once again this night, these people are proven correct.

Sometime after darkness falls I am dispatched to a neighborhood near the city's eastern border for a fairly routine call of shots being fired. Soon, though, the call begins to take the shape of something much more severe, much more troubling. Numerous calls are now flooding into Central Dispatch. There is a rifle involved. Someone is shooting at a car and the vehicle has crashed into a telephone pole. The car is now on fire and there may be people trapped inside.

I flip on my overhead lights and siren and maneuver my patrol car down East Genesee Avenue, falling in behind the patrol car of Officer Matthew Ward, a friend and co-worker who had hired on the same day as me many years ago. We arrive in the area within about 45 seconds of being dispatched and we can clearly see the fire from six blocks away. As we pull onto the actual scene, the front end of the victim's car is engulfed in flames from bumper to windshield, a telephone pole protruding from the engine compartment. There is a person, a young man, slumped down in the driver's seat.

We both act without the slightest hesitancy and for some reason this surprises me, even as we pry open the driver's side door. *This car could explode at any second* says the clear, but inaudible voice in my head. I give the voice little attention and focus on the task at hand.

Inside the car, the only things more intense than the heat are the driver's gunshot wounds and the blood they produce. As Matt and I try to pull him from the car, I wait - I actually consciously wait - for an explosion. I think of my new wife and wonder if she will still love me after I become disfigured by fire. I think about the things we do, the places we go, the vacations we take, and how that may all change any second. *This isn't fair to her!* my subconscious screams, but my mental vacation is short.

I am back inside the car now. Matt and I extract the driver with some effort. It takes less than a minute, but seems like an eternity, every second ticking away louder and louder in my head as I wait for my pending engulfment by flames. When the driver is finally freed we drag him to a front lawn, streaking blood along the pavement. The relief of being away from the burning car lasts for only a second.

"There's another one in here!" Matt shouts after going to check the vehicle's back seat. My heart sinks as I leave the first victim and return to the fiery hell that was once an automobile. Choking mildly on the smoke, I am suddenly physically exhausted, but also wired with adrenaline as I backtrack toward the flames.

You're pushing it now; you're really pushing your luck, my inner voice scolds. Again I ignore the voice just as I am sure Matt is pushing aside his own self-survivalist instincts. I am sure his inner dialogue is also screaming at him to flee. But that is not an option for either of us.

We begin pulling the second man from the rear seat. In my periphery I see a Saginaw Fire Department Inspector, who had been on fire prevention patrol in the area. He runs past with an extinguisher and starts, in vein, to work on the engine compartment. Flames hiss and dance against the black of night as they fight his efforts.

Sirens scream from blocks away as we try to free the man in the back seat. He too has been shot, and there is a pistol lying on the floorboard near his feet. The heat of the fire becomes more intense as the initial quelling efforts of the Fire Department Inspector have been futile.

Get the hell out of here! my brain commands as two more police cars scream up the road. A fire truck follows and several more emergency vehicles descend upon the intersection from various directions. But, inside this backseat there are just the three of us . . . and the smoke and the fire that threaten to consume us all. One final pull and we are free of the car, free of the smoke, free of the danger. *Thank God*, I think, as we drag the second victim from the wreckage and lay his limp body in the grass.

Red and blue lights shatter the darkness now. Wailing sirens fill the air. Suddenly there is a muzzled explosion. I turn quickly and, through the smoke, can no longer see the Fire Department Inspector. He is also my next door neighbor. For a brief second, I think about how to tell his wife he has been killed. Then he is visible again. He would later tell me how the tires on the car had blown out from the heat. He would then joke about needing to change his underwear.

By now, Halloween is a distant memory for this neighborhood. Tonight, the scary stuff is no longer pretend; the blood and screams are for real. Fire engines, ambulances and police cars clog the street. People - some carrying fire hoses and some toting medical bags - rush to do their jobs as a young man breathes his last breath and dies on a stranger's front lawn. The other man survives, although I have never been told, nor have I inquired, of his injuries or the extent of his recovery.

After being hired together in May of 1994, Officer Matthew Ward and I have remained the closest of friends. We never discussed this incident at length after it occurred, but I think we both know we cheated death this night, a night that remains one of the most vivid memories of my career.

On a wall in an office on the second floor of my home hang several awards I have received during my employment as a Saginaw police officer. A black-framed award with gold trim and a bright gold City of Saginaw seal recounts the events of October 31, 2000. The last few lines read as follows:

. . . *Upon arrival you found the vehicle in flames. Without regard for your safety you entered the vehicle and removed an unconscious victim who was slumped over in the front seat to a nearby yard. You then returned to the vehicle and removed a second victim from the rear seat. It was later determined that both victims had been shot and one later died from his injuries. Congratulations on a job well done.*

I have not worked a Halloween since.

"Frislee"

Even on an unbearably hot summer afternoon the streets can be a cold place. Dozens of times a day the thugs and gang-bangers shoot their icy "I'd-love-to-kill-me-a-cop" stares my way as I patrol the unforgiving streets of a dying city.

As a matter of survival my guard is always up. Every day my face reflects a mirror image of blank stares back at the hoodlums and soon-to-be murderers that hate me and the tiny sliver of balance I bring to the streets of urban America. The edginess and paranoia slowly eat away at what's left of my pre-cop persona, often spilling over into my personal life. My years on the streets, for the most part, have flushed me of trust and unabated friendliness.

Yet for sanity's sake, I have found even the most jaded cops long for those small victories - those moments of serenity - that become more and more elusive as the years slide slowly by.

I cannot recall if it was late August or early September. In Michigan, this time of year finds the seasons intertwined, like lovers wildly embracing on a park bench. The individual features of each are visible, but it's not quite clear to who each belongs. It was a sunny day with a temperature that, 20-plus years ago, would have found me hanging out at the beach.

Dangling my arm out the driver's side window of my patrol car, I round the corner of a little-traveled street on the city's far north side. The area cannot even really be called a neighborhood anymore. The calculator in my mind's eye tells me only about 20% of the original houses from these blocks still stand. The rest have long-since been demolished, leaving behind vacant lots and a green wavy lake of thigh-high uncut summer grass. A few other houses stand vacant and open for public viewing, the boards on their doors and windows having been torn away by drug addicts and homeless folks in their quest to escape the elements, or to escape reality with the help of a pipe or a needle.

My police radio has been quiet for nearly 15 minutes, an almost unimaginable time span during warm weather months. The temporary respite lulls me for a moment, but my mind snaps back to reality when I hear the screaming of children around the next block. I quickly pull around the corner to find they are not screams at all; they are the joyful screeches of three young black children, one boy and two girls, playing in the street. I stop for a moment and stare, dumbfounded, at the activity in which they are engaged.

They are playing Frisbee.

I grew up in Port Huron, Michigan, a waterfront community of about 35,000 people, straddling the banks of both Lake Huron and the St. Clair River. And, while my childhood home was modest, it was only about 10 blocks from the beach, where I spent my summer days with friends, often for 10 or 12 hours at a time. The beach was as good a place as any to hide from my own troubles, offering similar concealment, I suppose, as the vagrants find in the abandoned houses which now surround me.

Some guys spent their days playing hoops on the one basketball court Lakeside Beach had to offer. Others engaged in sandbar football games, or just walked around and talked to girls. But my friends and I were Frisbee junkies, spending hours throwing and catching - behind our backs, between our legs, or while spinning on one finger – the heavy plastic disc which was the sport's namesake. It was a white boys' beach activity if ever there was one. For me, chasing a Frisbee at the beach used to be as natural as chasing kids with handguns has now become.

When I get within view of the three children, they immediately stop and stare at me. Their surprised stares must have reflected mine because the last thing I expected to see today was three poor, black, inner-city kids playing Frisbee in the streets of this not-quite-yet-abandoned hellhole of a neighborhood.

The boy finally ends our staring contest and breaks into a broad grin as he runs up to my car.

"Hi, po-lice!" he says with no hint of disrespect in his pronunciation of my chosen profession.

"Hi, kid," I reply.

"You know what we're doing?" he continues.

"What are you doing?" I respond, awaiting an answer not quite as funny as the one I actually get.

"We're playing 'frislee!'" he says, his excitement bubbling over. "Do you know how to play 'frislee?'"

"Yeah, I've played a few times."

"Can you play 'frislee' with us?"

Without hesitation and without correcting his better-than-the-real-word pronunciation for the activity, I jump out of my patrol car and turn off my portable radio. "Sure." *I'm taking a mental health break.*

Immediately the two girls break their silence, run up and announce they want to play "frislee" too. Their brother is disappointed that his one-on-one "frislee" time will now be shared, but the disappointment is evident only on his face. He doesn't protest aloud.

The four of us spend the next 10 minutes throwing the plastic disc from one to the next. The kids clearly have not mastered the art of Frisbee throwing yet, as their tosses send me scrambling into bushes, tall grass and down the unoccupied street. Soon several adult relatives emerge from the childrens' modest home and watch in silence on the porch as their children play "frislee" with a cop. They do not say hello, but they also do not scold the kids to "Get away from that po-lice!" This is as close to a kind word as I get most days.

I look around as we play. There is no sand and no deep, blue lake nearby. There are no silently passing freighters to form the backdrop to this scene.

Here, years of poverty, violence and unemployment combine to paint a vivid portrait on the canvas of this once-proud blue collar neighborhood. This work of urban art can logically be called only one thing – Hopelessness. And it's been painted to perfection. But as I throw the disc one last time to the young boy, I realize there is a flaw in this "hopeless" portrait - the joy of three kids and a cop playing "frislee," if just for a few moments, on a worn urban street.

This is, by far, the best 10 minutes of my day.

When time allows during the next few weeks, I re-visit the neighborhood. Twice the children are playing and we engaged in brief "frislee" time again. Days later, though, the children are no longer outside, so I anxiously hang around down the street waiting for them to emerge, the way a young child might wait on his playmates on a summer day. I never see them again. Sometime in October I find their house, too, has gone abandoned and the family has moved.

For me, however, those moments of being at peace, playing "frislee" with three young kids on a crumbling street in a dying town, will last a lifetime.

I hope the children remember as well.

The Fall

Death comes looking for those who tempt
With evil in their hearts and souls unkempt
Lives surrounded with gunshots and flight
Until death finally finds them some deep, dark night

Last night had been a good night, a night when I felt
alive as a cop for the first time in months . . . hell, maybe in
years. But in law enforcement the good times are always
tempered by bad the times, and the bad times are never too
far away.

The City of Saginaw and the Saginaw Police Department had experienced a rare victory just a month ago.
The city's ever-present financial troubles had surfaced again
and this time would result in the layoffs of about 50 public
safety employees, 26 of them coming from the police
department. This was a nightmare that was previously
unimaginable for me. Our staffing at the time was 94 officers
– down from 165 just a decade ago. The job was hard
enough and dangerous enough as is, but cutting the officer
compliment by another 26 people was sheer lunacy.

I had recently become a member of the police union
executive board, and we spent the better part of the winter
campaigning for a public safety millage, which would put
both the police and fire departments on solid financial
footing for at least five years. Campaigning for this tax

measure was a Herculean effort and it was the last thing, as a police officer, that I ever expected to take part in.

I spent countless hours over a period of months sitting through campaign strategy meetings, working telephone banks in a musty union hall, and walking door-to-door on Saturdays, asking – in fact, begging – people to vote in favor of this millage. Physically, this effort was not overly taxing. Mentally, it drained every ounce of my enthusiasm.

The whole thing bugged the living hell out of me. This wasn't how I envisioned life as a cop. To me, knocking on doors and asking for money was unnatural. It made me feel dirty somehow, like the bums I see so often sifting through garbage cans looking for their liquor money one 10-cent returnable bottle at a time. I spent hours on front porches, debating the merits of this millage, debating the value of a well-staffed police department, debating whether these citizens should spend their money so I can risk my life every day in this rotting town trying to help them. None of it made sense.

Aside from beating the support drum to the citizens, we also had to muster financial backing. Running a campaign of this magnitude wasn't cheap. But eventually businesses, private donors and a number of officers and firemen, through personal donations, raised enough money to pay a tab that tallied in the tens of thousands of dollars.

The weeks before the actual vote were tense. I thought about my next career move and where I would go from here if the millage was turned down. I was not one of the officers slated to lose their jobs; I was not that fortunate. I was one of the cops who would have been left behind to struggle for survival in a lawless hellhole. Sheer chaos, I was sure, would grip the streets of Saginaw if 26 more cops headed to the unemployment line, and I was not about to put myself or my family through that horror.

We gathered the night of the vote at the Fraternal Order of Police lodge, a clean yet modest building used by officers for union functions, picnics and family gatherings. A big screen television in the corner drew most people's attention as a couple hundred of us - cops, firemen, spouses, politicians, business people and reporters – gathered to await word on the outcome; to await word on the very future of a city.

My wife and I sat anxiously as I gripped a can of beer I was too nervous to drink. The minutes dragged slowly past, but finally our fears were allayed around 11 p.m. when voting results came trickling in one precinct at a time. The millage did not fail. In fact, it passed overwhelmingly, receiving support in every one of the city's voting precincts. The proverbial public safety executioner would have to store his axe for another day.

This tax initiative and the income it promised led to overtime for directed patrols in a city that desperately needed its streets cleaned. So it was that yesterday I had felt like a cop again. Assigned to a six-man directed patrol unit for an evening, we were given the task of hitting the streets and, for lack of better terminology, fucking with every bad guy we could find.

Swarming in on street corners, the looks we got from the local thugs and dope-dealers were priceless. The bad guys in Saginaw barely bat an eye at regular patrol officers these days because they know the patrol division is too overwhelmed with calls for service to cause them much trouble. But, they knew when we jumped out in blue jeans, tennis shoes, equipment belts and "Gang Task Force" shirts that we meant business.

Our shift lasted a mere six hours, but they were six of the greatest hours I had experienced in recent memory. By day's end we had made five felony arrests, engaged in a couple car and foot chases, recovered two stolen vehicles and a handgun, impounded three other vehicles, and had written a slew of traffic and local ordinance violations. More importantly, however, we gained back some much needed respect for a police department which desperately needed just that.

That was yesterday.

Michael S. East

Today does not find me celebrating victories, but mulling one of those small failures that add up to a police career peppered with defeat.

Most summer days my dark blue uniform, equipment belt and bulletproof vest squeeze the energy from me within a few hours. My sweat-soaked undershirt sticks to my skin and I can feel the heat rise up into my face when I grab the top of my vest and pull it out from my chest, seeking a few seconds of relief from the suffocating swelter. It is a warm day in early June, but today a light early summer breeze softens the heat and puts me in an unusually good frame of mind for a work day.

It doesn't take long for my mood to swing.

Two other officers have requested assistance with a felony stop of a vehicle involved in shooting up a north-end housing project earlier in the day. The suspects – four punk teenagers with lifeless eyes and permanent, evil grins - are taken into custody without incident.

Numerous officers have arrived now and the street is flooded with cop cars and on-lookers that have to constantly be shooed away from the scene. The suspect in my back seat is only 15. He softens a little bit now that he's out of earshot of his companions. The answers to my questions come in the form of "yes, sir" and "no, sir," an unusual show of respect for a cop in these filthy streets.

I leave my suspect locked inside my patrol car and go talk to other officers at the scene. They have checked the suspect vehicle and no weapons are found, although the vehicle is sporting a few bullet holes of its own. You don't shoot up the projects in Saginaw without getting a few rounds of lead thrown back at you.

When I glance to my left, one of the suspects sitting in the back of another patrol car has slipped his handcuffs. His shackled hands are now in front of him and he has removed all the braids from his hair, changing quickly from cornrows to a large afro. Not knowing what kind of evidence we have from the previous shooting, he has changed his appearance in case there are witnesses. *Very resourceful*, I think to myself.

Unfortunately, there is not enough evidence to lock up any of the four. The vehicle, which likely fell into the hands of these kids through a trade for crack cocaine, is impounded. The officers holding the adult suspects identify and release them, watching as the thugs walk away from the scene with smirks on their faces, mumbling to themselves that it was "some bullshit" how they were treated.

I am not so fortunate as to be able to cut loose my catch. There are few things more frustrating or time consuming than taking a minor into custody. They cannot simply be released. There are forms to fill out and there is always the lengthy babysitting time to factor in before a relative agrees to come to the police station and pick up the child. I'm going to be stuck with my kid for a while. That doesn't bother me too much today, though. Maybe it is the kid's recent politeness, or maybe it is the cool summer breeze that keeps me from overheating on this warm day. Either way, I feel I can reach this kid and I am willing to give it a try.

We are at the police station within a few minutes and I am able to contact the boy's mother on the first try to come and retrieve him. Furthermore, mom doesn't sound drunk, high or confrontational; she sounds like an intelligent, caring parent. That is a rare commodity in my line of work.

The boy and I talk for a while as I gather information about him to complete a juvenile custody form. He remains courteous, but he has trouble making eye contact. I think he's actually embarrassed by his situation. This is a good sign.

Years ago I had given up trying to talk sense into violent juveniles. I found by the time most kids reach the stage of police intervention, their path in life has been laid and their destiny pre-determined. Too many times, I preached the common line: "You're headed to one of two places – jail or the grave." Too many times my counseling attempts were met with blank stares or a pointed "Fuck you, man." Too many times I have found these same kids lying dead in the street, or helped send them to prison as they stood in shackles in a courtroom and stared at their sobbing mothers, their young eyes pleading for help. And so I had given up, content to do my job, log my hours and go home. But today I am ready to try again . . . just one more time.

By the time the boy's mother arrives, we have established a decent rapport. The child's grandmother, a kind-looking woman in her 60s, has come also. After I explain what had transpired and her son's suspected involvement, I invite mom, grandma and the boy to sit at a table in the corner of the police station lobby.

Mom tells me her son is a good kid who has gotten mixed up in the wrong crowd. She tells me, though, that he has been "banging" since he was 12 years old and she can't get him away from the gangs. Grandma sits quietly, nodding her head in shame and disgust. I look at the boy and his mood is changing now.

I ask him to relax and just listen to what's being said. "These are people who care about you. They just want you to make something of your life and not be another statistic," I tell him. Mom speaks to him in a tone more caring than I could manage if I were her. The boy cocks his head slightly and then his body stiffens.

I intervene and talk to the child in a quietly firm tone, and he pays attention like he had in the holding cell. My words are reaching him. His eyes begin to water, and I think to myself, he needs to hear this from a man. He has no man in his life, only women. He's probably never gotten – like hundreds of other children and gang-bangers in my city – that fatherly guidance that can put a child on the straight and narrow.

The boy reminds me of another teen called Mick, who stoically sat through a similar speech from a cop years ago. Mick had his trouble with the police. His mother had pleaded with a cop for help years ago. The cop had reached Mick. Maybe this kid can be reached too. I talk non-stop for about 10 minutes. I talk about self-respect and pride. I talk about the value of education and growing up to get a good job and earning enough money to be self-sufficient. I talk about what a great thing he has in the two relatives who are sitting here right now that care for him.

He listens quietly, non-defiantly. He knows he's faltering. He knows he's falling. He wants to reach out; I can see it in his face. He wants to reach out; I can see it in his eyes. He wants help. He wants to be saved. I am reaching now, as best I can, with words and gestures and all the caring I can muster. There are a dozen other people in the lobby right now, but I don't see them. All I see is this kid, a kid who is about to fall. And I can see The Reaper, as he follows closely behind. This kid in front of me is not far from death, much like Mick was years before.

I stop talking and there is silence as he stares at the floor. I've reached him. And now I await his hand to grab mine. I wait for him to reach out and let me pull him back from the edge. I wait as the clock on the wall ticks. I wait as the people around us carry on with their lives. I wait as this child struggles to decide whether to save his own life. I wait for his hand to reach out for mine. The hand never comes.

The boy looks up at me and his mood has changed. There is only darkness. There is only hatred. He has composed himself and he's a thug again. He looks me up and down, pulls a bag of Skittles from his pocket and throws a handful into his mouth as a sign of disrespect. He looks away.

I am deflated, but try not to show it. This child and I are worlds apart. I am a white cop in a uniform. He's a young black kid from the streets. I have decades of history pushing against me. Today – again – I lose this game of life and death.

The boy's mother reads the defiance in her son's eyes and the subsequent defeat in mine. She rises, shakes my hand firmly and gives me a sincere "Thank you." Her shoulders slink lower as one more weight is piled upon her years of sadness and disappointment. "I hope I don't have to come down here again today," she says. "This is the second time I've had to pick him up down here."

I'm confused now. "The second time; what are you talking about?"

"The police had brought him down here this morning because he was with his cousin when his cousin got shot," she says. "I just picked him up from here eight hours ago and, look, he's already out running the streets, getting into trouble again."

I am totally dejected now. I know it shows, but I don't care. This is why I quit trying. This is why I decided to just go through the motions, punch in, punch out, and go home. It's just too demoralizing - too mentally draining - to care anymore.

"C'mon, let's go," the woman says to her son. He gets up, walks out the door and never looks back. He has fallen. I have failed.

The woman can sense my loss as much as I sense hers. She offers me her hand again, forces a slight smile and says simply: "Thank you for trying." The grandmother gets up, gives me a silent nod and walks toward the door. I write my name, badge number and work phone number on a piece of paper and hand it to the mother. "I'm sorry I couldn't do more. You call if you need me though."

Our eyes lock for a brief moment. Time slows to a crawl. The woman nods and walks out the front door into the streets. I never hear from her again.

Author's Note: In September of 2008, after learning of an outreach program offered through Peace Lutheran Church, I decided again to try and reach some of Saginaw's troubled children. The youth mentoring program at Stone Elementary School has again inspired me to strive to make a difference. Some days are more challenging than others. However, each mentoring session is a gift that allows me to see these children away from the streets that slowly consume them; it allows me to see them for who they really are – children. As of this writing three other Saginaw police officers have also become mentors and joined this program. I hope on some small scale we can make a difference. It took nearly three years, but I am ready to try again.

First on Scene

When I used to think about bigger cities like Detroit or Chicago I always told myself that I was glad not to be a cop in any of those places. To me, Saginaw, Michigan, with a more modest population, always seemed of a more manageable size, if not of a more manageable crime rate.

But as the years go on, I think maybe I would like the anonymity of a larger police department. Maybe then everything wouldn't be so magnified. Maybe everything wouldn't be so familiar. Maybe everything wouldn't be so personal.

For more than 15 years I have patrolled Saginaw's 18-plus square miles, hour after hour, day after day, year after depressing year. Every day I see the same sights and the same people repeated over and over, like a bad song that I can't shake from my subconscious.

Like many decaying urban centers, Saginaw is a place largely void of hope, enthusiasm and motivation. It is a city where legions of adult men wander the streets aimlessly, even on a midweek afternoon when most rational people are celebrating "humpday" on their workweek's mental calendar. Work is the farthest thing from the minds of a large segment of this city's population. Predictably, this nothing-to-do-and-all-day-to-do-it lifestyle leads only to trouble.

It is well after dark on a mid-January night when Officer Matthew Ward and I take a call for a double shooting on the city's southeast side. The location of the call is no surprise. The convenience store where the shooting is reported has long been a hotspot for gangs, drugs and gunplay. Right smack in the middle of a residential neighborhood, this store provides the only source of food, liquor, tobacco and other items for people who live in the area. Many of the store's customers are too poor to afford transportation that would carry them to a larger retailer farther away, so this store does a decent business. Dodging bullets is an inevitable part of the shopping experience, but at least it is closer than Wal-Mart.

The nature of the call is also no surprise. The first month of this new year is not even half over and these hard urban streets have already been bloodied time and again. In fact, my partner and I have the distinction of being first car on scene to two homicides already this year. Tonight will make three.

We cover the distance to the scene in just a few minutes. Maybe it is all the hot calls we have responded to recently, but our patrol car's red-and-blue top lights and wailing siren do little to stir my adrenaline tonight, even as we accelerate down the one-way street and close within a block of the shooting scene.

"Seven-forty-two, we're on scene," my partner informs Central Dispatch.

"All units hold the air for seven-forty-two," the dispatcher responds.

When we climb out of our patrol car, two men immediately come from behind an abandoned blue, two-story building next to the store. "He's been shot! You gotta help him, he's back here!" one man exclaims.

Matt locates a victim in front of the store and, as he tends to him, I follow the men to the rear of the building and find another victim, a man in his late teens, lying on the ground. I send the two men back to the front of the store and confirmed with Central Dispatch - mostly to follow protocol - that an ambulance is en route. The man is clearly dead and there isn't anything that is going to save him.

"Seven-forty-two, do you still need the air?" the dispatcher inquires.

I hardly think this guy is going to be disturbed by a little radio chatter, I think to myself, grinning slightly at my own inner voice comedy routine. "Negative" is my only response.

Sirens, some distant and some within a couple of blocks, fill the brisk night air. Through the wisps of my foggy breath I look closer at the man who has brought me to this place on this night. Being first car on scene Matt and I are going to be responsible for securing the crime scene, which means Dead Guy and I are going to be spending the next several hours together. I might as well get to know him.

The man is lying on his back with his mouth and eyes wide open, and his arms spread out like broken wings on either side. I start to check him for wounds, but I can find none. He is dressed in only a shirt and jeans, which is clearly not warm enough for a night like this. *Shoulda worn a coat, pal.* I don't think he planned on dying tonight, however, so I guess he can be excused for not dressing for the weather. *My inner voice comedian is on stage again.*

The man has no pulse. He is undoubtedly dead, but he has no visible wounds. Staring at him for a moment I think he reminds me of someone. Then it hits me – he is posed just like Jesus on the cross, his arms spread, hands palms-up to either side, eyes open, and his head slightly askew.

"Where's he shot?" Matt asks as he comes around the corner after talking to the less injured of our two victims.

"Not really sure. I don't see any wounds," I reply.

Then Matt points out a tiny tear in the left side of the man's shirt right near his heart. When we lift the shirt, there is a small bullet wound right above the man's heart. The absence of visible blood tells me he has bled out internally. "That explains the lack of blood," I say more to myself than anybody else. A couple other officers come around the corner accompanied by two paramedics.

"Hey, he looks like Jesus," one of them quips.

"That's exactly what I was thinking," I reply.

By this time the scene has been taped off to keep out the ever-thickening crowd of people who have come to gawk at the demise of the city's latest crime victim. Some officers take it upon themselves to scour the area for witnesses, a task that is often pointless. Others secure the perimeter of the scene.

The structure we are behind is an abandoned apartment building. I remember the first floor housed an ice cream shop several years ago. I recall now having stopped there years back with a couple officers for free ice cream that the owner had offered up. Those officers have since left Saginaw for other police departments. The ice cream shop has long since been abandoned as well. But I'm still here. Here with the bullets, the violence and Dead Guy.

The victim is lying in what used to be a parking lot, but it is hard to distinguish as such through all the garbage and broken concrete. Old clothes, fast food wrappers and other items are strewn here and there. An increasingly colder winter wind whips against my face.

The back of the parking lot used to be enclosed with a privacy fence, but that barrier is broken down in many places. People from the blocks to the east now use this route as a shortcut to the market so I will have to stay back here to keep anyone from walking through from that direction and disturbing the crime scene.

Moments later, the paramedics announce the man is officially expired. *No shit?* I think sarcastically. Everyone departs, leaving me alone again with Dead Guy and my thoughts. Looking down at him and pulling my jacket tighter against the stinging wind, I think absent-mindedly that he must be cold. This ridiculous thought makes me chuckle, but also reminds me of how quickly death can come – so fast the brain cannot even process the impending journey of the mind, body and soul.

The man, a man who in some respects still looks very much alive, *was* alive less than an hour ago. But his life, his story, and his future were stolen by a single bullet; taken by a bullet he probably never thought would come.

I walk slowly around the body while broken glass crushes beneath my work boots and garbage swirls in the wind. I feel an odd sense of compassion for the man, if only for the briefest of seconds.

After a while I grow tired of looking at Dead Guy and I walk around to the front of the market where the shooting had occurred. A crowd of people, oblivious to the cold, still stands on the other side of the crime scene tape, staring blankly at the scene. To my left, a detective interviews a bystander. Other officers mill about nearby in case trouble breaks out beyond the yellow tape.

Across the street, I see faces pressed against the windows of a retirement center high-rise building. These people, whose faces resemble prisoners peering out of a jailhouse, live in fear every day, their only immediate defense being a lone, unarmed security officer who patrols their building and probably hits the deck as quickly as the residents when bullets start flying. *What a way to spend your "golden years,"* I think to myself.

Looking north, I see people parking their cars blocks away and walking to the scene, toting small children with them. They are parading horrors around in front of their kids that they should be trying very hard to shield them from. I look at my watch. It's 10 p.m.

When I walk back to my post, Dead Guy is still there. I almost feel badly for leaving him for a couple minutes. I guess dead people aren't too put off by rudeness, though. I think back for a moment about all the young men I have seen murdered over the years. Some of them I have literally seen breathe their last breath. I wonder if they would change anything if they had it all to do over again.

Just then the brisk winter wind whips harder yet. I pull my jacket even tighter, and stiffen myself against the coldness I feel run through me.

Expect the Unexpected

I don't remember exactly what time of year it was; the incident itself was vivid enough to block out any recollection of seasons. The weather was mild and there was no snow on the ground so logic tells me it was springtime, or possibly late autumn.

My career as a cop has robbed me of many things over the years, the first of which was the relative innocence I still possessed in my pre-cop life. I've often heard that people change – become more guarded, more paranoid and less optimistic - after they put on the badge and uniform. As a matter of survival this change is an absolute necessity. Innocence must die for cynicism to flourish, and cynicism is a vitally important tool for survival in the streets.

But innocence is not the only thing lost. The streets have also stolen from me time – time and memories. Since May 1994 I've lost hours . . . days . . . months to The Job. Week after passing week I can look back and I have a hard time recalling the small things that happen in the streets – a wave from a child, a friendly hello from a stranger, or an unexpected rare smile from a random citizen. My weeks instead are punctuated by the hot calls, the homicides, the fights and the carnage of car wrecks. The small, uplifting moments simply wash away in the tide of insanity which is the life of a cop.

Some grains of good times – playing Frisbee with a child or the warm handshake of an elderly woman - do manage to stick in my mind's mental strainer. But for the most part my brain dismisses the fleeting positive moments for the sake of recalling and replaying the bloody vividness of all that is bad. These are the memories which must be kept sharp, and recounted in detail in police reports, on the witness stand and at family gatherings, where friends and relatives always want to hear the latest play list of crazy human behavior. These are the same people who quietly whisper behind your back about how much you've changed since becoming a cop.

This would be a day, like so many, that was punctuated by a single event. Nothing else about this day would stick with me, lost forever in the muddle of what transpired on a random street, in a house where I rushed in to "protect and serve" and walked out an hour later shaking my head in disbelief.

The call relayed to me by Central Dispatch is for shots fired in a block on Saginaw's east side. This is a place where gunfire is as predictable as the rising of the sun each day. Dispatch advises they are being told two men are shooting at a car. As usual, nobody directly involved in the incident is calling. But I am close enough to the venue that my heart starts beating quickly and causes my eardrums to pound with the sound of pumping blood.

Within seconds I am in the area, far ahead of any backup that will be available. Immediately, I spot two young teens walking down the street mid-block. I have no idea how, or even if, they are involved so I approach them with caution, handgun drawn, but behind my right thigh at the ready.

"Seven-thirty-four, I'll be talking to two mid-block," I advise the dispatcher.

"Talking to two mid-block. All units hold the air."

The two teens come to my car when called and put their hands on the hood, which indicates to me they are not involved in this incident, or at least they no longer have guns. Had they been toting iron, they would have darted from the street between houses, over fences and across fields at the sight of my patrol car. Nobody cooperates with one lone cop when they're carrying an automatic felony in their waistband. Still, I try to keep them off guard with conversation as I check them both for weapons.

"You guys been out here a while?"

"Naw, just a bit," one teen responds as I reach around to check his front pockets and waistband.

"You hear any shots being fired?" I ask while checking the small of his back. It's not the normal hiding place for handguns – too hard to reach for in a pinch – but I check anyway to head off any potential surprises. His answer is enough of a surprise in itself.

"Naw, but they said a woman dead up in there," he responds as calmly as if he's telling me the time.

A befuddled "What?" is all I can muster.

Neither teen has a weapon. Both are facing me now. The silent one remains silent. The other points to a small house less than 150 feet away, a house I know to have a past history of drug and gun activity.

"They said a woman dead up in there," he repeats, maintaining his calm, nearly bored, tone.

I dismiss the two as I turn my attention toward the house – toward the threat I had just had my back to. "Central, how far off is backup? I'm being told there's a dead woman in a nearby house."

"Still a couple minutes off," one officer replies into his radio ahead of the dispatcher's inquiry.

How long ago was this a dope house? My mental rolodex offers no answer. I have not had an arrest here this year, but there are so many dope dens in Saginaw, it's hard to keep up on the current status of each unless you work in the drug unit. And even then knowing the status of an individual drug house week by week can be a crapshoot.

I walk toward the house now, gun still drawn at my side. I try to stay in line with trees and anything else that will offer cover should someone come out shooting. Down the block the two teenagers don't bother to look back as they amble away slowly. The voices of the dispatcher and other inquiring units gets lost now in the inches separating my

69

shoulder mic from my ear. The adrenaline is pumping and I am focused only on the house. I have tunnel vision now – I can feel it. The only two things in the world are me and the house. People are watching but I don't see them. Birds are chirping but I barely hear them. I walk within 50 feet, 40 feet, 30 feet.

Grab a tree and wait for backup, the Voice of Reason whispers in my head. I do not hesitate. I move forward as I continue to focus on the house. *Backup will be here soon enough. There's something going on in there and you have to go in,* responds the Hero Cop in my head. It's the Hero Cop voice that so often gets cops killed. I hate the Hero Cop voice. Always have.

On the porch I listen briefly at the front door and window. Sobs from inside. Sobs and muffled, tear-choked pleading. *You have to go in now! She could be dying!* my Hero Cop sidekick implores. I push open the door in what feels now like slow motion.

"Saginaw police, c'mon out!" I shout. The sobbing continues but nobody appears. I make quick entry, gun first, and scan a tiny living room. Nobody. The sobs and commotion continue from a room to my left. I breech the door and find several people in the room crying around a woman lying motionless in her bed. A young man is trying to talk her back to life. A teenage boy sees me and runs from the room to the back of the house. He is crying uncontrollably. The scene comes back to real-time now as my brain lets in the outside noise.

"Seven-thirty-four, how are you doing?" an anxious dispatcher inquires.

Police and ambulance sirens scream up the block as the man looks pleadingly toward me. "Help her, pleeeeeease."

"Central, we need medical in here now!" I call into my portable radio.

As if filling their roles in a real-life stage play, two paramedics rush in on cue. Several cops follow. The man is pushed away from his girlfriend's body as we try to find out what happened to her. The man says she hadn't been feeling well. He left for a while and when he came back he found her unresponsive. "Please help her!" he screams, tears flowing full force now.

Medical bags and cases are opened one after another at a furious pace as paramedics grab various objects – the tools of their trade – and put them to work to revive the woman. Wrappers are discarded and thrown around the room. More officers have arrived. But with more officers come more people; more people who want to come into the house and interfere, people who want to be a part of the drama even though they have no connection to what's happening here.

Officers outside push back the curious as I brief my sergeant on what I know so far. Outside the tiny bedroom comes loud screams followed by more yelling. We dart into the living room and find officers restraining the teen who had earlier run from the bedroom. In the mayhem he has grabbed a knife and is trying to thrust it into his abdomen. We restrain him during a fight that lasts too long as family tries to intervene, and paramedics continue to work on a woman who is probably already dead.

Outside the house, the cops argue with angry on-lookers who somehow think the police have caused whatever is going on here. Distrust of the police is a way of life for some, even during times like these when our task is simply to keep the way clear for medical personnel to try and save the life of someone who may be their friend or neighbor.

Inside the house, the knife-wielding teen has been restrained and family has taken over the task of calming him. Inside the bedroom things are not going as well, although to the untrained eye – to the family – it appears the woman might have a chance of survival. The paramedics work feverishly and are now trying to prepare the woman for transport to a local hospital. They have to give her every possible chance.

And in the midst of the confusion, the yelling, and the crying, I conduct interviews with family to try to uncover more clues as to what happened. In the end, the situation turns out to be of a medical nature. The woman, now either dead or near death, had nothing to do with the report that I originally responded to that gunshots were being fired.

I step out onto the porch as the woman is being loaded onto a stretcher for what I think is a pointless ride to the hospital. Within seconds a car screeches up and a man jumps out leaving the door open and the car running. I can see the intensity in his eyes. I have seen it before. Here comes another fight. He leaps the front stairs three at a time with anger – *why always anger?* – in his eyes.

There is clearly no reasoning with this man right now and he reaches the door full throttle, bolting his way through three cops and making his way inside the front door. He starts screaming as he is tackled and handcuffed. Someone says he is the woman's brother. Attempts to calm him are useless as he continues to fight to try and get to get at his sister – the woman we are trying in vein to save.

When the man is taken outside to a patrol car, the crowd begins to yell obscenities and scream anti-police rhetoric. The scene has grown so volatile that every cop in the city is here now. Here at this house. Here at a place where no crime has occurred, but violence threatens to boil over.

Amidst the mayhem, paramedics are trying to get the woman out the front door and down the steps to a waiting ambulance. In their hurried efforts to get the stretcher out the door, a sheet that is covering the woman slips, exposing one of her breasts. Family members immediately start screaming at the paramedics . . . at the cops . . . at each other and the crowd . . . about how poorly the woman is being treated.

"Man, cover her up! Don't take her out there all exposed! Ya'll don't even know what you're doing!" yells one family member, directing his voice more at the anxious throng outside than at the people he is admonishing.

She's dead, I think to myself, I don't think she really cares.

Officers at the scene have to form a wall on either side of the stretcher to ensure safe arrival at the ambulance as we walk the gauntlet of angry bystanders – the people doing everything they can to ensure we can't do everything that we can for this woman.

The scene reminds me of a similar one I had worked about two years after I started employment as a police officer. That day, dozens of friends and neighbors had rioted after an elderly woman had died of natural causes. During the mayhem, as family pulled the woman's body from the stretcher, and cops handcuffed and threw to the ground people from the volatile mob, I was scuffling with an angry teenager when I looked over my shoulder to see another officer fighting off a 12-year-old girl who was on his back and trying to pull his gun from its holster. The "what-the-fuck-is-going-on-here?" expression on the officer's face hangs on the walls of my mind to this day. He quit his job shortly after that incident. Just like now, that day 12 years ago was one of the times I, too, seriously thought about calling it quits.

"What do you want to do with this guy?" my sergeant asks now, pointing to a patrol car where the woman's brother had been taken after being handcuffed inside the house. It's my scene so the guy's fate is up to me.

"Do you have a preference?" I ask.

"No, I don't really care," he responds. "I'll leave it up to you."

I talk to the man for a short time, the man I had fought with only 15 minutes ago. He has calmed now and the fire of hatred in his eyes has been extinguished, replaced now by the painful realization that he has lost a sibling. When I remove my handcuffs from the man, he quietly apologizes and begins to walk sullenly toward his family. Then he stops, returns to me and shakes my hand. The welcomed gesture is totally unexpected.

Almost as unexpected as the events I experienced responding to a call for shots fired a short time ago.

Michael S. East

Author's Note: More than a year after this incident, while off duty and filling my vehicle at a local gas station, a woman in her 40s approached and asked if I had any money I could give her. Her eyes were sunken and tired; her shoulders slouched under the weight of some heavy, unspoken burden. My normal, abrasive response to people begging money never surfaced that day. I could sense this woman was different from others who have begged cash from me in the past; somehow I could sense the depth of her despair. As I opened my wallet and handed the woman the few dollars I was carrying with me that day, she began to cry and told me how her life had come unraveled in the past year . . . when she unexpectedly lost her daughter to a heart-related illness. She described the house where this incident occurred. The woman didn't know me. For once I was not a cop; I was simply a random stranger in a random place, put in a position to give comfort to someone I did not know. "She was my baby, and now she's just gone," the woman lamented as tears flowed down her cheeks. I never told the woman I was there when her daughter died. As she hugged me tightly and thanked me for the four dollars, I struggled for words to ease her pain. "It'll be okay," was all I could think to say, even though I knew it was a lie.

Karen King

I never met Karen King, but I will never forget her.

Karen's name and her image – a smiling, carefree photo that appeared in the newspapers after her murder – still make unscheduled cameo appearances on the stage of my mind. To me, her name is synonymous with one word. That word is failure. That failure is mine.

Karen King was an 18-year-old Michigan State University freshman, who died a brutal, unimaginable death hours after being abducted outside a Saginaw convenience store on January 3, 1997. I'm sure there have been more since her, but Karen is the first person that, as a police officer, I consciously am aware that I failed to help.

The night of Karen's death was not unlike most others. My 3 p.m.-to-11 p.m. patrol shift was not unusually busy. I was working a beat on what at that time was the quiet part of town – Saginaw's west side. The blue collar neighborhoods of this area had been in decline for several years, but it was a slow decline - a decline, I remember thinking back then, that might even be reversible. This night's events would hasten that downward spiral.

Karen had been home for holiday break from college when she made an ill-fated decision to go to a neighborhood convenience store to buy ingredients for the family's taco dinner. Karen King left home on January 3, 1997 at about 6:15 p.m. She never returned.

Unbeknownst to Karen, she was about to fall victim to the utter senselessness that grips the streets of the city I try so often in vein to protect. August Williams, then 25, and his then-15-year-old cousin, Shytour Williams, set off for the same destination as Karen that night, apparently armed with a flare gun wrapped in black tape. They were about to unleash a night of horror unthinkable even by Saginaw's appalling standards.

At 7:41 p.m. Karen's father called Saginaw County Central Dispatch to report his daughter missing. Unfortunately, calls for missing teenagers are common and this report did not generate an abnormal amount of attention from the handful of officers working that night. The magnitude of this incident would not become apparent until about 8:15 p.m. when a caller reported seeing two men force a woman into a Chevy Blazer at the store where Karen was last headed. The caller, however, had waited more than an hour to report the incident. By this time Karen's ordeal was in full swing.

Reports of what happened to Karen prior to her death vary somewhat, but the basics of that night are pretty clear. After forcing Karen into a vehicle, the Williams cousins reportedly drove her around Saginaw, as she was terrorized, tortured and raped. At one point the pair was alleged to have driven Karen to a residence on Saginaw's east side, displaying her to some other people, showing her off like a trophy as she begged for her life. Nobody made an attempt to call the police. Nobody intervened. Nobody helped.

Like my co-workers that night, I spent the next few hours unsuccessfully trying to locate Karen and the Blazer. By shift's end I had hoped for the best, but deep in my subconscious, expected the worst. Maybe the next shift would find her unharmed. Still not knowing the horrors of Karen's final hours, I had even hoped the whole kidnapping scenario was one huge misunderstanding. But there was no misunderstanding. There was no happy ending. The sigh of relief would never come.

When I arrived at work the next day, I learned this day did not exist for Karen King. A few hours before my afternoon shift began, two passers-by found Karen's lifeless body lying near a scrap yard on Saginaw's east side. The remains of a promising young girl had been unceremoniously dumped here; her once bright smile vanished like the shine on the now-rusted metal in the scrap yard not far from where Karen's body lay discarded.

The news of Karen's death hit me harder than I expected. The details relayed to me by detectives of the horrors Karen endured during her final hours still haunt me. Had I looked a little harder, had I been a little more diligent, had I taken a different route during my search, I might have changed Karen's fate. But I did not prevent this atrocity. Karen is dead. And I failed.

Later that month witnesses finally stepped forward, offering help that was far too late to do Karen any good. Soon both suspects were arrested. I was working when Shytour Williams was taken into custody. It is a day I learned to hate much more deeply than I thought I could.

The trial of the Williams cousins was reported to be emotional and somewhat racially themed (the Williams cousins are black, King was white). I did not attend any of the court proceedings, choosing instead to choke down whatever information was offered by the local newspaper. Even those stories I could only digest a little at a time. Both August Williams and Shytour Williams are currently serving life sentences.

The market where Karen was abducted is yards away from a small restaurant where I used to eat breakfast in 1994 while in training on the midnight shift. I used to think of the restaurant – referred to by cops as simply *eleven-eleven*, because of the address of the establishment – as a warm, inviting place, with its greasy all-day breakfasts, knotty pine interior and eclectic customer base.

The restaurant has long since closed, and the surrounding neighborhood is now far from warm and inviting. "For Rent" and "For Sale" signs dominate the neighborhood. Karen's murder was a random act of violence so appalling it changed the landscape of an entire neighborhood. Many fled the area for safer suburban locales. Drug dealing, shootings and homicides are now quite common in this neighborhood where families once grew. Young teens, their pants sagging low and their facial expressions more dull than their futures, litter the street corners now, spending idle time wasting their lives away, trying to look tough while waiting for their hopeless futures to arrive.

I sat in a bar recently with a cop who was hired with me in 1994, and we discussed Karen and her murder over a pitcher of beer. Marking the 10-year anniversary of the event, the local newspaper had run a series of stories about Karen's murder; stories which forced me to re-visited memories that had gathered some mental dust; stories which forced me to scrape the scab off wounds that I suppose will never totally heal.

"Yeah, I read it," said Brian Lipe, a light-hearted guy in his 30s who makes a point of rarely showing emotion. "It made me cry," he finally admitted, as he sheepishly searched for composure in the bottom of his glass.

Surprised by his candor, I quickly looked away and waved to the waitress for another round. But, in my mind, a mental sigh of relief washed over me. I did not voice it, but the thought was there. *I'm glad I'm not the only one.*

"Yeah," was the only response I could muster.

The Bungalow Motel

He doesn't say anything as we pull into the parking lot. I think to myself that he is too unemotional, too detached, for a guy who experienced so much in this very spot. But I don't voice this observation. This is not my memory. It's not my place to trample it with the sound of my own voice.

I've always known Officer Denny Howe to be a good, no nonsense cop. And while we've both worked at the same police department for about 15 years, I never really worked directly with him much until a change from eight- to 12-hour shifts threw us onto the same shift assignment and days-off rotation. We've talked often since – about police work, people, relationships and politics. But the most intense conversations we've had revolve around the place that surrounds us right now – The Bungalow Motel in Inkster, Michigan.

An incident 20-plus years ago at this non-descript spot along Michigan Avenue first caused me to take notice of law enforcement and the depths of the sacrifices made by those who choose this profession. What happened in this place – the brutal murders of three policemen I never heard of before July 9, 1987 – has been seared into my memory ever since. The fates of Officers Danny Dubiel and Clay Hoover and Sergeant Ira Parker also, I believe, turned up the volume on that inner voice that beckoned me toward the field of law enforcement.

Michael S. East

In July of 1987 I was eight months removed from college graduation and was wandering blissfully through life, trying to find a job as a newspaper reporter. I finally accepted a sports writer's position with a small daily newspaper in mid-Michigan. The job paid only $13,000 a year and I recall thinking that, with some sacrifice, I could survive on this nominal salary. Even as I mulled over my own trivial thoughts of money and budgets in 1987, Officer Denny Howe was learning much more about sacrifice than I might ever know.

As we glide slowly through the parking lot of the Bungalow Motel, I remain quiet. We are on the way to Detroit from Saginaw to pick up a prisoner, but a quick detour after dinner at a nearby Italian restaurant has brought us here to meet the ghosts of Denny's past. It's August 2007, but – and I can read this clearly in his eyes - it is 1987 for Denny as we embark on a tour of the dusty, dark attic of his past. Judging from the forced stoic expression on his face I don't think he's been here in a while.

In 1987, Denny was a cop here in Inkster prior to returning to his hometown of Saginaw a few years later. I had told Denny on a couple of occasions I was interested in writing something about the Bungalow Motel ordeal for an upcoming book I was working on. The deaths of those officers had stuck with me over the years and I wanted to know more about what happened in this poor, violent community of 30,000 people on the outskirts of Detroit. Eventually, one spring evening a few months back as the two of us guarded a homicide suspect, we had several hours to kill. It was during this conversation that Denny re-lived for me the events of his previous cop life in this city where he lost his police virginity. The details were startling.

"The first night I got to Inkster I go to a breaking and entering in progress with Tom Freeman. I get there and a guy was shot in the arm, but his arm was in a coat," Denny had recalled. "His arm was hanging by a piece of skin. When I pulled off his coat his arm severed.

"Another day I pull up to the back of a building and get out of my car and this guy's propped up against the wall with his head cut off and it's sitting right next to him. I never found out why, but obviously it was an intended hit," he had continued. "We also went through a time when there was this guy scooping up prostitutes, stripping them down, tying them up in abandoned houses with phone cords and setting the houses on fire. I think we lost eight or nine prostitutes to him."

Denny had recounted these stories with amazing clarity as he pulled them down, one after another, from the bookshelf of his mind and read them aloud to his eager listener. Being a police officer in Inkster, Michigan, I soon learned, took a quicker toll on some officers than others.

"There were roughly 35 cops or so in Inkster, but I would see it go as low as 11. I would see them come and go – some in one day. They would leave after their shift and you'd never see them again," Denny said. "And I always got the shit. They used to say 'Howe's working today; somebody's going to die.' People would hang themselves, or cut their wrists in the bathtub. One lady got hit by a bus. Have you ever seen anybody get hit by a vehicle that large? She was literally turned to mush. She had no form. She was like a huge bag full of water."

Back in present time, I gaze now around the parking lot of the Bungalow Motel. Inkster may have provided my partner with some vivid memories, but none were as tragic and violent as the ones he has of this place. Denny absent-mindedly points to the exact spot where shot-up patrol cars had been parked that fateful day 20 years ago. He shows me where bullets pierced the doors and walls of nearby buildings. He points to the motel office and says bullets lodged inside the safety glass that protected the front desk clerk. He speaks in specifics, rather than generalities, as if he is still looking at the bullet holes and the carnage that engulfed this place in the summer of '87.

This is not the first time we've discussed the Bungalow Motel, but it's the first time I've seen him confront his demons face-to-face. Denny Howe is one of those cops who always wear a crisp uniform accented with highly polished shoes. He always gives special attention to his appearance. He is always well-groomed and impeccably manicured. Yet right here, right now, he is disheveled. For a few brief moments, Denny looks unclean. He looks like he *feels* unclean. This is a place in his life he can never groom into perfection. It's a place that will never be mentally tidy.

I break my attention from Denny, inhale a deep breath and look around more intensely at the place where so much transpired so long ago.

The call, I think, must have seemed as routine then as most of the runs I respond to now. Newspapers reported that officers Danny Dubiel and Clay Hoover were sent to the Bungalow Motel to serve a bad check warrant to Alberta Easter and Roy Lemons Jr. And, while the warrant was for a felony offense, it was still thought to be nothing unusually serious. When the officers arrived at the suite being shared be Easter, Lemons Jr. and two other men, George Lester Lemons and William Lemons, things went bad in a hurry. Sergeant Ira Parker was thrown into the violent fray a short time later.

I think back to when Denny had recounted the incident to me some months ago with an even tone and a blank stare. The car is silent, but Denny's words play now in my head like some sort of subconscious color commentator highlighting the horrors of that day with lively descriptiveness.

"Ira Parker got called at the station by Booker, the hotel maintenance guy. Booker was a nice guy, but he liked to tell stories, and he observed Dubiel and Hoover sitting on the end of the bed and he could see they were disarmed," Denny said. "He called down to the department, but they didn't take him seriously. He called a second time and Ira Parker went down to the motel.

"The door was shut when he got there and they shot him when he came in the door. What happened was they shot Parker. From what I understand, Dubiel rushed the one who shot Parker – shot him dead in the door – and they shot Dan, I was told, in the top of the head. At that time Clay ran to the corner of the room. He was asking: 'Why are you doing this?' And then they killed him too."

Denny recounted that at that point all anybody knew was that there had been shots fired at the motel. Nobody knew the condition of the officers. The suspects, playing it off as a hostage situation, holed up in their rooms throughout the night as police tried to negotiate a deal for the release of Dubiel, Hoover and Parker.

I look now as Denny quietly points out to the door to the actual rooms where this nightmare unfolded. I try to imagine the scene as I remember more of our previous discussion.

"I was on my way to work when I heard them talking about it on the radio and I saw the state police go whizzing by," Denny had recalled. "It was chaos. Lots of people and news crews. It (the shooting scene) reminded me of a sporting event the way the people were cheering . . . against the police.

"Everybody was there. You had Novi, Northville, State, County, Garden City, Wayne, Westland, Detroit, and Troy. They came from everywhere. There were a lot of cops there. It was quite an ordeal. It started at about 5:15 pm . . . I was there for quite a while, then I would go out and take calls because they were backed up, then I came back."

I remember Denny sighing slightly before he went on as his frustration bled through 20 years of mental fabric.

"You got tired of the waiting, the bullshit. It was not an organized scene at all. We thought about rushing in, but we were trying to be careful because there were other agencies there. It would have been a slaughter," he had said. "They were heavily armed. They were going to do something big. They had guns, gas masks, ammo.

"We kept asking on the phone to speak to the officers. They kept saying they were locked in the bathroom. At one point one of them muffled a voice like it was the officers through the bathroom door, which we knew then we were in trouble. You knew they were dead. You just knew. There was way too much gunfire. Too much. They would come out and just spray the parking lot with rounds."

I snap back to present day for a moment and sneak a quick look at Denny. His eyes are hollow. I recall how Denny told me the ordeal had ended with the suspects surrendering at about 3 a.m.

"After it ended I would not go into the room. I was there when they brought the bodies out – I had to be there. I had the right to, but I couldn't go in the room. That's a memory I didn't want.

"We didn't talk about it a lot afterward. At least I didn't. I can remember not wanting to cry because I'm not a crying person. I remember getting a phone call from my mom and dad because they wanted to make sure I was okay, and I didn't want to cry. They told me to quit and come home."

Denny, who remained an Inkster cop until his life's work brought him to Saginaw, stares for a moment now at that door and at the threshold he never breeched. I recall how he once confessed he felt invincible when he started out as a cop.

"Prior to this happening I felt I would never get hurt and people I worked with would never get hurt. I was stupid. Obviously we can die any day. It's up to most people if they want to make it our last day. Citizens can make it our last day. A set-up – it can be a barking dog complaint, a parking complaint," he had said. "There was a point in my career – and you've got to remember I was a fairly new police officer being exposed to a lot very fast – when I just got tired of seeing all the death. We had shootings and suicides every day."

I think now Denny does not feel invincible anymore, but I sense he is at peace with that fact. Conversely, the past 20 minutes have made me feel more vulnerable to death than ever before. Like an oversized jacket, it's a feeling that doesn't quite fit me. Not yet at least.

I often hear people describe police officers as being arrogant and unemotional. But as I make my way down this often surreal career path, I think more and more that being arrogant and unemotional is the only way to deal with the life we lead. And maybe, just maybe, it's an attitude that's earned and not necessarily learned.

Most cops I know perpetually carry the mental burden of the fights and the blood and the death and the gore that is their life. It's not an easy load to shoulder. Denny Howe's mental burden is heavier than most.

Our stop at the Bungalow Motel ends quietly as we drive back past the office. Denny notices that a word has been added to the motel's name and he points out it has a new color scheme. The name change and new colors – a dingy grey and flat teal – may have dulled the past for some, but I can see in Denny's eyes that these memories will never lose their sharp edges.

And as we pull onto Michigan Avenue and head eastbound toward Detroit in silence, I know Denny's mind must still be exploding with memories of July 9, 1987.

I have experienced many things in my cop life. I hope I will never experience the depths of the anguish he felt that day.

The Sentinel

Every day when I pull into work, get out of my car and walk toward the doors of the Saginaw Police Department, I leave hope behind. Hope and optimism have taken an extended vacation in my working world and I don't expect they'll be back anytime soon.

And so starts another day of mayhem and madness that was unthinkable to me less than two decades ago. On the Monopoly board of life Saginaw, Michigan, is the equivalent of Mediterranean Avenue . . . without the amenities.

The weight of being a Saginaw police officer pushes down on me day after day, slowly crushing what's left of my desire to make a difference, while snuffing the flame of law enforcement dreams that was ignited in the police academy so long ago. As I have traversed the mental peaks and valleys of my career, I have learned that cops often must dig deep in their souls to find the people, places and things that offer even the slightest bit of happiness. And sometimes that fleeting moment of hope has to sustain us for an awfully long time.

So it goes as I pilot my patrol car one afternoon through Saginaw's First Ward District, a part of town whose rich history is keenly offset by its bleak present and dim future. A vast expanse of train yard slices through northeast Saginaw and forms the southern border of this ramshackle part of the city. And while much of Saginaw festers with the wounds of abandonment, the decay here is noticeably accelerated.

History has it that during Saginaw's automotive hey-day, trains brought workers – mostly transplanted southerners – to Potter Street Station by the hundreds and the thousands. They came looking for work in the many factories and foundries that dotted Saginaw's north side. And work was plentiful in this automotive hotbed.

Factories buzzed with activity as the work force tried to keep up with demand. Getting a job back then, I am often told by local old-timers, was as simple as asking. Rooming houses were bursting at the seams as Saginaw welcomed wave after wave of migrating workers. That was a long time ago. The assembly lines have long since gone silent. Potter Street Station, its windows boarded over and its platform now quiet, today sees only the shadows of vagrants and vermin.

As I drive up North Sixth Street, all prosperity has vanished from these parts. Fifth and Sixth Streets are a set of two-lane, one-way roads that cut underneath the rails of the train yard and Interstate 675, providing easy non-stop access up and down the north end of town from Janes Street to North Washington Avenue. These two roadways were a hub of bars, gas stations and businesses in better times. They look now like the bombed out roads of some third-world country, rather than main traffic arteries of an American city.

I drive past a couple crumbling, boarded-up gas sta-tions that slowly rot in the afternoon sun. Up the road a party store, a Laundromat and a rib joint keep a weak pulse for an abandoned business district hovering near death. Prostitutes of various shapes, sizes and colors have replaced the money spending consumers that once roamed these avenues. The one-way streets and lack of traffic lights make this a good place for men to pick up their whores quickly and escape without drawing the attention of the few cops who patrol this beat.

Farther north the business climate changes from sex to drugs. The scantily clad hookers have given way to the saggy pants crack dealers that ply their trade from block to block, running up to passing motorists to trade rocks of cocaine for $20 bills. Certain street corners have stayed hot with crack dealers during my entire career, while others go cold from month to month, as the dealers switch locations like mobile drive-thru restaurants serving their dope addict customers.

It is in these neighborhoods that I am most comfortable being a cop. I have worked Saginaw's northeast side for the better part of 15 years and I have become familiar with all of its intricacies, in terms of both people and geography. Through simple repetition it has become easy to figure out the routes and habits of the drug dealers, the whores, and the purchasers of both services. The gangs, for the most part, have also remained constant, with the faces changing as members enter or exit prison, get murdered or come of age and officially pursue violence, their life's only logical course. Some of the gang members I deal with now weren't even born when my career started.

The game continues day after day, week after week, year after year - good guy hunting bad guy, bad guy killing bad guy and, occasionally, good guy simply becoming bad guy. It is within this scenery that I find the unlikeliest of motivation on this day.

I had met the woman before and had, at first, considered her nothing more than a nuisance. She called to complain quite frequently about the drug dealers that constantly hung around her front yard. More often than not her calls would wait for a long period of time before being answered. By the time the police responded the drug dealers usually had moved on.

On several occasions the woman had waved me down and complained about the drug activity that plagued her tiny corner of the world. Quite honestly, her complaining bored me. The drug peddlers outnumbered the cops in this neighborhood about 25 to one on any given shift and we had more pressing - more violent - calls to deal with. The only real solution for her was to move, I had thought to myself, although I never gave voice to the thought. That was something I could not bring myself to say, even on my worst day.

More recently, though, I had begun to appreciate the woman. Looking back I think this appreciation grew more out of my maturing as a cop than it had to do with anything she had said or done. She had not changed. She had always been a sentinel of hope in this neighborhood. For the most part, she stood alone here against evil, much the same way I often feel alone being a cop. Maybe I just realized I owed her more than I was giving.

The woman's house is well-kept and sits on the western edge of what used to be the Daniels Heights Housing Project, a massive expanse of generic two-story, multi-unit brick buildings that extended across the city's north side. "The Projects," as they were called, were a hotbed of activity when I got hired. Crime was so rampant there that a federal grant covered the cost of three officers – a sergeant and two patrolmen – to tend to the law enforcement needs of just the housing complex.

During summer months especially, dope dealing, gunplay and neighborhood riots were so common that I sometimes was called there six or seven times a shift. So it was that I smiled generously when I heard this housing project was being torn down in the mid-90s. It was to be replaced with more attractive townhouse-style homes that were supposed to mark the revitalization of this neighborhood.

I drove through the projects quite often as the demolition was in full swing. Bulldozers knocked down walls, exposing to the public the guts of the buildings where I had seen much blood spilled. This entire small city disappeared within several months, leaving behind nothing but vast vacant fields and the memories of roads like Ray-Jac Place and Whittington Street. To the east, Leon Scott Drive – named for the first black Saginaw police officer killed in the line of duty – remains intact, but now is bordered by a few crumbling basketball courts, busted up picnic tables and rusting grills that sit unused and rotting. All that is left of the projects are the memories engraved on the minds of those who might remember.

After the demolition was complete something unexpected happened . . . nothing. The government-funded redevelopment that was to follow never occurred. Federal funds dried up and the families displaced by the demolition of this housing project never returned. There was simply nothing to return to.

The woman's front porch this day offers little more than a view of block after block of vacant land. The children all left. The parents all left. The grandparents all left. The drug dealers did not.

I see the woman today, standing on her front porch waving at me. Although I have never asked, I think she is in her sixties. She is always dressed tastefully, if not modestly. She is always smiling. *God, how can she always be smiling?*

When I pull up curbside and get out of my patrol car she immediately comes down off her porch, reaches over her chain-link fence and greets me by grasping my extended hand with both of hers. Her touch is warm and friendly, not too much unlike her smile.

"I'm so glad to see you," She says, as she proceeds to tell me about the latest group of thugs that have been using the corner by her house as their sales counter. She describes them in detail, including their height, build and what colors they're wearing. She even tells me where they place their lookouts who yell out "po-po!" upon sight of the police.

I realize now, maybe for the first time, just what a strong woman she is, standing out here in broad daylight giving descriptions of the gang-bangers that torment the peaceful life she is trying to live. Conversing with the police is a dangerous pastime for anybody in this neighborhood, but she continues talking with sincerity and conviction. "I have lived here since 1960," she tells me. "I'm not going to let these drug dealers intimidate me. No sir."

As we talk I look around. There are maybe five or six dozen houses in a 10 square block area surrounding the woman's house. A block to the east is a party store where gang members love to hang out. The last of the old auto plants still operating on the city's north side looms like a giant behemoth two blocks away, its smokestacks poking up over the treetops behind the woman's home. This neighborhood, like the city it is a part of, appears to be beyond hope.

The area has always been attractive to the drug dealers because of its proximity to North Washington Avenue, a large thoroughfare well-traveled by drug buying customers from Bay City, Essexville, Reese and other towns to the north and east of Saginaw. It's a goldmine for dope-slingers and they're not giving it up.

Neither is this woman.

We continue to converse for some time about the neighborhood and how it has changed over the decades. She gives me a complete history of the area, but her story grows gloomy as she talks about the past 20 years. Crack cocaine, it seems, has effectively killed the neighborhood she talks about with such conviction.

Looking around again, her yard is well manicured and flowers grow along the side of her house. She has a chain-link fence to offer some protection from the drug dealers. It is only four feet high and can easily be scaled by young men. Still, she keeps the gate padlocked in what I see as a symbolic sign of defiance.

She tells me how she has had a couple of stray bullets hit her house over the years. At least she assumes they were strays. One never knows the cost of "snitching." Last week, somebody egged her front porch. She was sure the drug dealers did that, more to be annoying than intimidating.

After a while I am dispatched to a call. I tell the woman I have to leave and I thank her for talking to me as I vow to keep an eye on her as often as possible. She thanks me in a soft and sincere tone. Then she says something I do not expect. She grasps my hand again with both of hers and looks me straight in the eye. "I know you police are very busy," she says. "But I love you all. You're my angels. You're my guardian angels, all of you." There is not a hint of sarcasm in the woman's voice, only respect and compassion. Her words have carried me often over the years.

I continue to pay extra attention to the woman's house after this day, stopping to run young punks and thugs off her corner as often as possible. Most amble slowly away, cursing me under their breath. A few are arrested. Always, like cockroaches, they return.

Each time I speak to the woman, she thanks me for doing my best for her. She continues to call me and my co-workers her "guardian angels." I never felt I lived up to the title.

Eventually, one of our talks leads to the news I thought I would never hear. The woman tells me she is leaving. Her family has finally had enough. They worry about her constantly and they have convinced her to leave Saginaw and move in with them in safer city many miles from here. A few weeks later she is gone.

A couple years after the woman left, a private investor built new townhouses and ranch-style homes on the land vacated by the Ruben Daniels Housing Project. The area, however, is still plagued by numerous problems with drug dealing and gang violence. A block from her home one half of a new two-story duplex now sits burned, the reported work of area thugs who, as an alleged act of revenge, set the house on fire one night and waited outside, shooting at the house's occupants as they fled the flames.

This repetitive and escalating violence draws me back here a dozen times a shift, and even now I drive past the woman's house quite often. It sits silent and empty as the drug dealers roam freely on her corner. A "For rent" sign is taped in the window. Both the gate lock and the woman are gone.

And one less sentinel stands to fight the good fight.

Concrete Evidence

As a cop working the streets of a violent, poor and largely under-educated city, I find most days inevitably produce at least one new and bizarre experience. It's a part of the job I have just come to accept. Most of these stories tend to be forgotten, their vividness fading as the years, the people and the calls for service pile up, clogging the space in my mental storage bin. Some days, however, produce experiences so fantastic that my mind refuses to let them dull. This is one of those days.

It is late afternoon on a crisp, clear early autumn day as I pull into police headquarters to drop off some paperwork. When two other officers are dispatched to a call not far away, I do the polite thing and disregard one of the officers, volunteering to fill on the call for him. I will soon regret this decision.

Workers from a social services agency have called for police assistance trying to locate a man in his mid-20s who suffers from cerebral palsy. He is supposed to be living with his mother at a home on the city's east side. Relatives have complained to agency workers that they have not seen the man in a year or more. Now it's time to look for him.

The house where I am dispatched sits on the southern end of what used to be a thriving downtown Saginaw. The area was once popular among the city's many lumber barons - rich men with obvious rich tastes, who pulled many of Saginaw's financial strings some 100-plus years ago. The houses on this block are mostly three stories high and consist of varying architectural styles. While none of them are pristine, some are in relatively good shape. The one eye sore on this block is the house I now pull up to. Like a single dark cloud pasted against the backdrop of a deep blue sky, I can immediately sense a foreboding presence about this place – an unmistakable air of wrongness that I cannot quite define.

When I arrive, Officer Kelly Schmidt is already talking to social workers. They say the missing man's mother told them the man has been staying with relatives in another county. The caseworkers, however, say they've checked with the relatives, who insist they have not seen the man.

The next logical step is to search the house where the mother lives and the missing man formerly lived. The mother offers no resistance and gives us permission to search her residence to look for her son. This proves to be a nearly impossible task.

The three-story brick home is more than a century old and looks to be well over 4,000 square feet in size. Like many of the older, larger homes in Saginaw, it has out-lived its intended use and it has been sub-divided into apartments. The home is in terrible disrepair. There is neither electricity nor running water. The mother of the missing man is also the only resident remaining in the building. Everyone else has moved out, presumably fleeing ahead of a pending condemnation order.

The search will take a while so I summon a sergeant to the scene. I explain the situation to him and he never breaks from his "why-did-you-have-to-call-*me*?" smirk. Eventually, he accompanies Kelly and I up to the house.

Darkness is setting in and it is getting colder as we step over crumbling red bricks and loosened boards, and climb a set of stairs onto a large brick porch. Written in white lettering across a window near the front door, is an ominous message: *Prepare ye the way of the Lord.* A sudden chill shoots down my spine, and takes up residence at the base of my tailbone.

In the downstairs entryway, the stench of mold, mildew and urine combine to assault our senses. Still, we make our way upstairs, passing several locked and blockaded doors that we are told lead to apartments no longer being rented. In the apartment of the building's last remaining resident, a few candles illuminate the living room, exposing cockroaches that skitter here and there upon our arrival. We find no sign of the missing man in the apartment.

Next door is another apartment the woman says she uses for storage. We enter and find it stuffed with appliances, boxes, clothes and assorted garbage. Looking around for a starting point, I set off for what looks to be a bedroom. There are a few garbage bags full of clothes in a closet. In the corner of the room, boxes and small appliances are piled neatly about four feet high on top of a makeshift bed. The rest of the room is empty.

When I start for the pile of items in the corner the mother of the missing man breaks her silence. "That's all my brother's stuff," she says. "He stores it here 'cause he ain't got room at his house. Put it back neat when you're done."

Checking through the pile, I find nothing unusual. Unexpectedly, the woman breaks open the three garbage bags which had been sitting in the closet. "You want to check these?" she says, dumping the clothes on the floor. An overwhelming, suffocating smell of old urine immediately fills the room. Neither the pile of clothing nor the items piled atop this bed appear capable of concealing a body, so I retreat to the smelly kitchen, trading one bad stench for another.

We locate no sign of the missing man and move downstairs, where we find a stairway leading to the basement. The sergeant at the scene tells us he is going outside to radio for a police dog to assist in the search. When he disappears into the now chilly evening breeze, Kelly and I decide the basement is the next logical place to search.

The basement staircase is littered with garbage and halfway down we are slowed by piles of junk covering the entire bottom half dozen steps. It takes some effort to scale the obstacles, but we manage to literally climb *into* the basement, where we are greeted with a three-foot-high wall of discarded items covering almost every square foot of this level. Wheel rims, lawn mowers, television sets, stereos and boxes and bags of every size and shape stuff yard after yard of the indoor junk pile. There are several doors within reach, and there appear to be several more beyond the vastness of garbage, but they are unattainable. As we look at each other in disbelief, no words are spoken between me and my search partner. Words are not necessary; the scene speaks for itself.

In the corner is a window, but it is barred from the outside. I push open one of the doors that is within reach and find the adjacent room also filled nearly to the ceiling with broken items and discarded trash. I can barely comprehend the transition of this building from a large family dwelling into what it has become.

Suddenly, my flashlight begins to dim. I had meant to recharge it yesterday. The scene is straight out of a horror movie – searching for a body in the dark, dank bowels of an old, nearly deserted mansion. My skin begins to crawl.

Fire! The word suddenly appears on the mental movie screen of my mind. There is no way out of this dungeon, except for the cluttered staircase that brought us here. If a fire were to break out in this house right now, we would be trapped. Something is definitely wrong within these walls and a fire would be a great way to cover up the mystery. Outside, several relatives of the missing man have gathered. God only knows who is involved with the man's disappearance, but I would rather ponder that question from the safety of the front lawn. Kelly takes very little convincing when I suggest we retreat from the basement and await the arrival of the K-9 unit.

The brisk breeze outside is a welcome change and we are both relieved to be free from the grips of the house. Exhaling another breath of fresh air I look around and see the missing man's mother is sitting alone on the grass in the darkness.

I find a spot near the woman and sit down next to her on the slightly sloped lawn. She is obviously nervous as I begin to talk about her son and what could have happened to him. The woman avoids eye contact, but the angle of her shoulders, shoulders that appear to be bearing a burden far too heavy for her slight frame, tells me she knows the answers to the puzzle we are trying to piece together.

I soften my voice and press on, gently prying back the nails that hold in place the story she is trying hard to keep boarded up inside her head. After about 10 minutes, the woman begins to cry and I sense she wants to tell me something. Finally, I ask her directly if her son is dead. The answer is a somber "Yes."

The woman's shoulders rise slightly as she shrugs off the weight of her secret. She takes a moment to compose herself and then trudges on with her story. She says her son has been dead for about a month, but he was not murdered; he died of natural causes. She tells me someone – she won't divulge their identity - threatened to harm her if she told the police.

My mind is brimming with questions, but I don't ask them; it is better to let her speak on her own terms, at least for now. The woman eventually says she does not know where her son's body is located. I think I am not getting the whole truth, but she has gone silent again and I stop the conversation there. With this new information, the sergeant at scene instructs me to take the woman to police headquarters.

The situation has grown much more serious and the wheels of departmental policy now start in motion. A detective supervisor is contacted and he subsequently summons two detectives to the scene. They will take at least half an hour to arrive. We are also still awaiting a K-9 unit to continue the search.

Back at police headquarters, I sit with the woman as she sips a bottle of cola I bought for her from a vending machine in the lobby. She says she hasn't slept in days. Her bloodshot, sunken eyes scream exhaustion. She cries for a while and then falls asleep with her head on a desk.

About an hour after our arrival at police headquarters, the K-9 officer arrives and asks to speak with me in the hallway. He recounts the details of his search and asks if I had checked a bedroom in the second apartment upstairs. I tell him I had, but found nothing, although I retreated from the room when the missing man's mother dumped three garbage bags full of urine-soaked clothes on the floor.

The officer relating the story is visibly upset by his findings. He pauses momentarily, and then continues. I had actually been within a few feet of solving the mystery of the missing man. Had I continued to dig through one more layer of junk on the bed in the corner, I would have found what the officer and his dog eventually uncovered.

"He was on the bed," the officer says, "underneath all the junk."

My mind rewinds through my search of the room and the stack of items piled on top of the small bed. Everything sat flush. Everything was stacked neatly. There was no way a body could have been concealed underneath the smallish boxes and other items.

But it was there.

Lying directly on top of the bed, covered by neatly stacked items, the K-9 officer and his four-legged partner found the outline of a small man, turned sideways in the fetal position.

"But I don't get it. How could I have missed him," I respond. "And what do you mean 'an outline?'" Then comes the answer – the answer I don't anticipate, the answer I barely comprehend, the answer I will never forget.

"He was covered in concrete. When he died, somebody poured concrete over him and just left him there in the bed," he responds.

It takes a moment for my mind to register what I have just been told. I am still trying to frame a mental picture of the man as the officer continues on. He tells me the concrete had long since hardened. But apparently the cement job had been rushed because scattered around the cement-encased cadaver were the remnants of hundreds of long-since-dead maggots, which had presumably made a meal of the deceased man's flesh.

Before leaving the K-9 officer tells me they are awaiting the arrival of a specialist to crack open the concrete tomb. "It will have to be done carefully," he says. *Where do you train for that type of job?* I think to myself as I thank the officer for passing along the information.

After digesting what I have been told, I return to the room where I had left the woman sleeping with her head on a desk. God only knows what kind of dreams she is having.

Later in the night, detectives arrive to interview the dead man's mother. I leave the woman in their care and call my wife, telling her not to wait up as I settle in and begin writing the gruesome details of the case.

By 1:30 a.m., I am on my way home, replaying the previous hours and the day's horror show in my mind. In the early morning hours, I sit alone on my sofa, absent-mindedly watching the television, but not really paying it much attention. Four bottles of beer fail to clear my mind of this day's events, and a single simple thought finally creeps into my head: I am happy to be starting a vacation soon.

Sleep does not come easy this night.

Author's Note: The house mentioned in this chapter still stands vacant and looks as dark and intimidating today as it did the day I first entered inside its crumbling walls. To my knowledge nobody has ever been charged with a crime relating to this incident.

Cause for Celebration?

The days since I became a cop have provided a steady infusion of surreal moments. Not the least of these came during late spring 2007 when I was, through the benefit of a voluntary overtime assignment, asked to "participate" in a local high school prom celebration. It was one of those nights that puts an exclamation point on all that is wrong - terribly wrong -with the community that I am charged to police.

Springtime by no means has the monopoly on violence in Saginaw. But graduation and prom season seem to provide an informal springboard into each year's summer bloodshed. What I grew up to know as a time to celebrate one of life's small milestones is now known to me as an early death knell for those who will perish during the upcoming summer months.

And so on a warm summer afternoon I sit in a humid locker-room at the Saginaw Police Department and joke with other officers about the evening's assignment. Briefing is still half an hour away so we are in no hurry. I pull on my bullet-proof vest, tuck in my uniform shirt and buckle on my nylon gun belt (the nylon gun belts are a better fit with the more tactical uniform the SPD recently transitioned to. Its lightweight design is more comfortable than its leather predecessor and puts much less stress on my lower back, which has been ravaged by years of toting around pounds of cop essentials). I absent-mindedly listen as several officers joke about the absurdity of our task. Like most days, I don't bother to polish my boots.

Today's assignment takes me to Saginaw Township, a community partially born of Saginaw residents trying to escape city life during the past few decades. Saginaw Township now is home to about 40,000 residents and borders the City of Saginaw in various places on the north, west and south. If population trends continue, the people who landed here in search of more land and newer housing than the city has to offer will someday outnumber those who stayed behind.

Saginaw Township offers a fairly high-quality refuge for those tired of the urban problems which plague Saginaw city. The township is home to several bustling business districts, numerous restaurants and a large retail mall. And, what the township lacks in history, architecture and urban flavor, it more than makes up for with a vastly lower crime rate, lesser taxes and lower insurance rates than its urban counterpart. After 11 years of city life, this trade off eventually was enough to coax me to sell my previous home and move my family away from the city.

Today's briefing is being held at the Saginaw Township Police Department (STPD), a clean and orderly building about two miles from the city limits. The differences between the STPD and the Saginaw Police Department are distinct. Put into television terms, he STPD seems the equivalent of a military-haircut, hat-always-on-straight, no-joking-allowed episode of *Adam-12*, while the Saginaw Police Department more resembles the chaotic, two-day-beard-growth, uniform-shirt-unbuttoned set of *Hill Street Blues*. Considering Saginaw city's blue-collar background, I would say each department mirrors the clientele it serves.

Pulling into the department parking lot, my partner and I joke about how new and clean the township police department's patrol fleet looks. Conversely, our city police car checks in at well over 100,000 miles, and every mile announces itself through creaks, rattles and a less-than-tight steering system.

We enter the building through the rear door and are led through fairly pristine confines to a large upstairs briefing room. The room is slightly humid, but there are no foul-mouthed felons chained to the wall and there is no temporary holding cell reeking of urine and body odor. "This is niiiice," I quip to my partner as we say a few hellos to the officers who have already arrived.

There seems to have always been a bit of an ego clash between the Saginaw Township Police Department and the Saginaw Police Department. Some STPD officers have confessed that they think Saginaw cops are crazy to work in the city, drowning day after day in the violence and apathy of urban Saginaw. Conversely, STPD officers are often referred to as "beach boys" by my co-workers, a tongue-in-cheek jab at police officers that spend their years experiencing only the sunny side of law enforcement. Truth be told, the ideal job would be a mix of both departments. There are STPD cops who would love to experience the non-stop adrenaline rush of city crime. On the flip side, there are city officers who would die for the perceived calm of life as a township cop, pulling traffic stops at will instead of running call to call to call to serve a largely ungrateful populace.

Over the years a few city cops have fled the Saginaw Police Department for employment with the township force. Two officers I met early in my career had several years as city cops and made the jump to the township environment. Neither still works at the STPD, and talk was that they were too entrenched in the city police mindset to make a smooth transition to suburban policing. A few other city cops have tried to follow the same path, but were refused employment. The running joke was that these officers were considered too tainted by city policing to handle life "on the beach." I have yet to hear of a township officer applying for employment with the city department. Through it all, however, officers from each department have built a good rapport and seem to maintain an air of mutual respect, a respect that serves both departments well during weekends like this.

The event today in the township is nearly a mirror image of one which was held yesterday in the city. Agencies from around the county have agreed to chip in with manpower and both events are well-staffed; *too well staffed,* I think to myself as I sit through a fairly routine 20-minute briefing. We are here today to make sure the local high school kids – the prom goers and their friends and enemies - don't kill each other. The purpose of our assignment strikes me as a monumentally sad indication of the time and place in which I live.

Last night's prom at the Saginaw County Event Center (SCEC) had gone smoothly enough. Nobody was killed. Nobody was shot. Hell, I didn't even hear of a prom-related car-jacking. That's something for parents to be proud of.

Of course there's a reason things went so smoothly. Two hours before prom time found 52 police officers roving city hotspots and positioning themselves at various points around the venue. These numbers did not count the dozen or so other cops, myself included, that were working regular patrol shifts responding to calls for service throughout the city. These were all cops being paid overtime wages to make sure the city's youth didn't break out their weapons and punctuate prom season with a shootout.

There was a buzz throughout the city most of yesterday afternoon. Police cars from numerous agencies littered downtown intersections. Overhead, a Michigan State Police helicopter hovered in the skies. Atop a five-story parking structure across the street from the SCEC, a SWAT team sniper readied for long-distance intervention should gunplay break out in front of the venue. And while this presence - and the taxpayer dollars it cost - seemed like overkill, sadly, it was not altogether unnecessary.

Less than a year prior to this event I was one of a dozen or so cops assigned to the same venue to patrol outside that year's prom. Teenagers – people so young they can still be called kids - rolled up in pimped-out cars and SUVs, paraded around in pastel-colored tuxedos and dresses, and eventually made their way to a red carpet as family members played paparazzi, flashing photos by the dozen. On-lookers jockeyed for position, shoved each other, screamed obscenities and acted like complete idiots. All because someone they knew was going to prom.

I recall marveling at the absurdity on that day last year. What lessons were these kids learning? Is it really wise to teach teenagers to praise materialism, boastfulness and self-absorption instead of humility and a quiet sense of pride? The answer to these unspoken questions had come in the form of gunfire.

Less than 100 feet from me a teen pulled a handgun and started firing shots into the crowd. Hundreds of screaming and scattering people streaked across my sightline as I drew my 40-caliber Glock from its holster. Through the mayhem I had frantically tried to locate the fleeing suspect as garbled radio traffic sliced my eardrums through my shoulder mic.

Hoping to escape in a maze of aging and dilapidated homes, the suspect ran straight east into a nearby neighborhood. The foot chase ended a few blocks later where the teen, apparently driven to gunfire by seeing someone in the crowd he did not like, was cornered and taken into custody without officers having to fire on him. Back at the prom moments later, over-dressed teenage kids began pulling up to the venue again as cameras flashed and on-lookers returned to their vantage points as if the gunfire had never happened.

And so it was that yesterday 52 officers, a sniper and a state police helicopter were deployed at taxpayer expense to make sure last year's mayhem was not repeated.

Later last night, after many of the prom-goers had dispersed, some of the throng of officers drove into nearby drug areas to finish out their shifts rounding up bad guys. A joking co-worker challenged me to go to the north end of town and pull a traffic stop just to see what kind of backup would arrive. And so I did, quickly finding two out-of-town crack addicts cruising a dope neighborhood, looking for a score. I could not contain my laughter when, within 30 seconds, a helicopter was illuminating my traffic stop from overhead while five marked police cars stopped to assist. *So this is what it's like to work with proper backup*, I had thought to myself less than 24 hours ago.

Tonight the city's other high school has a prom scheduled. And while the venue has moved to a conference center in Saginaw Township, the police response will be very similar. After briefing, my partner and I head out of the Saginaw Township Police Department and make our way to a convenience store for cold drinks before heading to our post. As we joke about the expense involved in this operation, I tally up the two days' costs in my head. "What kinds of people live like this?" I say aloud to my partner, expecting nothing more than the silence he offers.

Then I look to my right and see a familiar corner as we round a curve and pass a street that separates Saginaw city from Saginaw Township.

My mind flips into rewind mode and I quietly recall a chilly night a few years ago. It was on this corner that I had stood alone in a silent salute as the body of Officer Jennifer Fettig passed by in a hearse. Fettig and her partner, both Detroit police officers, had been shot to death in a brutal, on-duty double murder. That night, her remains were brought back home to Saginaw for the next day's burial. I recall the surge of emotion I felt as I stood at my spot in the gauntlet of cops who stopped to pay homage to this slain officer. I also recall glancing across the street where a woman, her toddler and her teenage son also stood in silence. When the hearse had passed the silence was pierced by a loud voice.

"Man, I hope all ya'll motherfuckers get killed," the woman's teenage son had screamed at me. The woman held the hand of the toddler as she stood silently beside the teen, a slight grin visible on her lips.

Those are the kinds of people that live like this, I think now.

I never responded to the teen that night. His ignorance deserved no recognition. I did, however, attend Officer Fettig's funeral and stood by as her body was laid to rest.

Even though I never knew her personally, I found it hard – once again – to hold back tears when hundreds of white gloves snapped in salute, the rifles of the honor guard popped nearby, and the bagpipes played in my head.

My mind returns to present day and the task at hand as my partner pulls into a shopping center parking lot where we are to monitor passing prom traffic. Looking up and down the six-lane street where we are posted, I see some businesses have roped off their parking lots in anticipation of trouble. It is not unusual for prom goers and their entourages to gather by the hundreds in whatever large spaces are available, where quite often guns are flashed and fights break out. It looks like most businesses are trying to avoid this problem.

Several times the state police helicopter reports large groups gathering in parking lots on the city's east side. The groups eventually break up and begin their trek westward toward their destination. In my mind the police radio traffic sounds eerily like weather reports, tracking a dangerous storm moving slowly, ominously in our direction.

Everyone knew when the storm hit.

The sound of thundering music is a prelude to the arrival of the prom crowd as the first of hundreds of cars ride by. Most pass unchallenged. Others, however, can not resist the opportunity to ass-up and drive like maniacs while passengers hang out car windows, mocking the police presence. These persons are immediately pulled over and ticketed. As usual, common sense is at a minimum.

People complain throughout the night, sometimes vehemently. But the complaints that I hear are that the police are being too restrictive. Not one person complains to me about how sad it is that this show of force is necessary. Nobody complains about the burden the weekend's events are placing on the shoulders of taxpayers.

For the most part, my partner and I get involved in very little throughout the evening. It doesn't take long for the overwhelming police presence to keep most people in line. The few traffic stops we do initiate result in a handful of tickets and a couple of warrant arrests – nothing major by Saginaw standards.

The weekend's newspapers say relatively little about the police presence at the two proms. There is no outcry about the cost of containing violence. There is no call for parents to be more diligent in raising their children. The end result of years of unmitigated violence, it seems, is apathy. The cost of apathy, as I can attest, is repeated violence. In Saginaw, Michigan, this is the cycle of life.

My night draws to a quiet close around 1 a.m. In the end, nobody gets shot this night. In the end, nobody dies.

And isn't that what prom night is really all about?

Calm Before the Storm

It looks more like a bombed-out husk of a building in some terrorist-infested land. In actuality, it is another crumbling structure on Saginaw's northeast side. This building just happens to be a church - a house of God. I marvel silently at the splintered wooden front doors, which stand wide open and frame a full-on view of tipped over pews, assorted garbage and a crumpled altar. The roof had caved in long ago.

My eyes fixate on the tattered shingles and wood and my mind draws a parallel: this roof tumbled down like so many lives of so many people in this neighborhood, buckled by the weight that the evils of the streets have heaped upon their shoulders. "Even God has fallen on hard times in this town," I say quietly to myself, looking around seconds later to ensure nobody is listening. The streets are empty.

The call volume on this hot, summer afternoon has been steady but not overwhelming. This welcome pace offers time to meander the streets and take in the sights, the sights of decimation, dismay and decline; the ever-present signs of urban decay.

Three blocks away I guide my patrol car past another burned-out frame of a church. What's left of the building sits half underground and half above ground, giving the appearance of an abandoned bomb shelter. Gang graffiti is slathered across the walls. Two years ago a young child quietly confessed to me that her brothers – gun-toting teens that roam the neighborhood peddling crack while preying

108

upon anybody weak enough to rob – often store their pistols inside this church when patrol cars hit the block.

Hiding guns in a church. Now that's irony, I had thought that day. The act didn't surprise me; not much does anymore, not since I became a cop well over a decade ago. If nothing else, the streets of urban America are where I learned that evil - formerly an abstract concept in my adult life - indeed has a face. It is the face of man.

Not far away a fresh arrangement of flowers marks the spot where an old man was murdered last summer . . . or was it the summer before? Hard to keep them straight sometimes. Three blocks away a cross and more flowers mark the site where another body dropped. On Veterans Memorial Parkway sit more flowers. At South 15th and Hosmer another fresh arrangement brings back memories of Halloween, a burning car and two more bullet-riddled bodies. The ghosts of those I have seen murdered litter the path of my daily travels. Memories of lives lost bubble to the surface as I drive, coaxing back to life the now nameless, generic faces of victim's with whom I have shared time.

I pass the next several hours this day in similar fashion – touring a city I have toured a thousand times while shagging a few radio runs and shooing the dope dealers off the corners. Daylight gives way to evening, which gives way to night, and by midnight I am hoping for nothing more than the quick arrival of 3 a.m. and the end of my shift.

In my job, though, hope comes with a price tag, and the cost of hope is usually disappointment.

"Thirty-seven-fifty-three, we've got one failing to stop," announces a state police trooper who is working a directed patrol assignment in the city. His presence is part of a cooperative effort that puts several state troopers inside city limits throughout the week to concentrate on pro-active crime suppression.

"Thirty-seven-fifty-three has one refusing to stop. All units stand by," a dispatcher repeats.

I am only blocks from the trooper as I punch the gas pedal and head up Sixth Street to join the chase. Within blocks I fall in behind the state police car as it turns in front of me in pursuit an older truck with a stove bouncing wildly in the truck bed.

"Thirty-seven, I'm behind the state unit. I'll call out the chase," I inform Central Dispatch as I tail the shiny blue MSP car with the single red overhead light.

During pursuits it is customary for the second in-volved police unit – if that luxury presents itself – to call out the chase over the radio. This tactic allows the driver of the lead car to concentrate on vehicle maneuvering without the distraction of using the microphone to give geographical updates.

"Thirty-seven, turning westbound Kirk from Sixth."

Central Dispatch echoes my every report for the benefit of those vehicles either paralleling the chase or trying to catch up to us. I am too focused on the task at hand, however, to give the dispatcher's voice much attention.

"Southbound Fifth coming up to Wadsworth."

The pickup gains speed as it cruises through two stop signs without braking. The truck is old, the suspension appears loose, and the driver is far too erratic. On the flip side, the state police car, with the benefit of a better engine, better maintenance and much calmer pilot, has no trouble keeping pace with the fleeing suspect. *This guy will be caught soon,* I think. Only the circumstances of the apprehension are in doubt.

"Southbound Fifth passing Johnson."

It's shortly after midnight and the two-lane, one-way street we are traveling is essentially void of other traffic. A few blocks later we approach a red light at the intersection of South Fifth and Janes Street. As I call out the location I know the suspect has no intention of stopping for the light. Fortunately, another state police car is stopped at the cross street, blocking that path. The truck barrels through the light without hesitation. Nobody is struck, but the second MSP unit inches forward to enter the chase, causing me to swerve left and lose my concentration for a few seconds as we head westbound on Thompson Street. The suspect has accelerated and as I tried to regain control of my vehicle, I fail to call out our change of direction. The mistake nearly proves fatal.

Up ahead another city officer, thinking we are still traveling southbound, is crossing a main intersection, trying to parallel the pursuit. As the cop crosses Thompson Street, the suspect roars through the intersection, the high-sitting truck's front end missing the driver's side door of the patrol car by mere feet. The barely avoided high-speed, t-bone collision most certainly would have killed the officer.

"Central, he almost hit me!" the cop shouts over his radio, clearly shaken by death's near miss.

I call out now that we are westbound on Thompson as the near tragedy shakes my nerves. The other state police unit pulls ahead of me as my own car's age and condition now factor into the chase. Several blocks away, I hear a loud crash as garbled yelling fills the police radio airwaves. When I arrive on scene seconds later, there is a three-car crash and the suspect's truck is sitting on top of the front half of the state police cruiser.

The next minute or so is frantic. The suspect is not finished fighting by a long shot. His truck is propped up on top of the police car and is teetering at an awkward angle. The stove lies in the street nearby. The man fights wildly as we try to extract him from the vehicle, throwing punches and resisting as he curses through the blood spilling down his face. The driver's door won't open. The man is large and combative and keeps reaching around the truck's cab while fighting off attempts to pull him out. Finally, an officer deploys a taser. It has no effect. The man eventually tires himself out and a half dozen of us are able to take him from the truck, get him onto the ground and handcuff him while he screams obscenities.

By now a couple dozen people from a nearby apartment building have come outside to investigate the commotion. Some gasp at the man as he lies on the ground bleeding from the crash and the scuffle that followed. Blood bubbles from his mouth as he screams, among other things, that he is an undercover cop. Most of what he says appears to be drug-induced gibberish.

Twenty feet away, the officer who just cancelled a date with death paces back and forth, his shaky hand holding a cigarette. I am glad my rookie-like mistake didn't kill him. Later in the night when I confess my fuck-up, he holds not even the slightest hint of a grudge. "Don't worry about it. I just assumed you guys were still going southbound. Then I see this big-ass truck coming right at my car. Man, I gunned it and he just barely missed me," he says. He lets out a nervous laugh – the laugh of a man who just cheated fate; the laugh of a man who is glad this night went his way because he is not prepared to die just yet.

As we mill around the scene, seeing who needs to do what and re-telling the story of the chase, Central Dispatch puts out a stream of not-stop calls waiting to be answered. As so often happens, one big event – this chase – is seemingly all that is needed to squash the night's calm. Reports of fights, domestic assaults and disorderly drunks clog the airwaves. The streets are coming apart at the seams . . . again.

I clear from the crash in fairly short order and head for a drunken disorderly call in a popular Westside bar district. Dispatch has received a few calls from different bars, complaining about the main drunken combatant, who was bloodied in a fight with a bouncer. The drunk also has called from a nearby pay phone, claiming to be a victim and asking for police help.

When I arrive, Officer Denny Howe has encountered the drunk, a man in his early 20's who has clearly had far too much to drink. The drunk tells his story for us and the other couple dozen or so people who mingle around the fringe of our comfort zone, looking for some additional late-night entertainment.

The drunk's story grows old quickly and Denny tells him to grab a tree as he checks the guy for weapons before putting him into a patrol car. Maybe it's all of the people hanging around, or maybe it's the fact we are still coming down from the rush of the previous car chase, but neither of us see, or at least mentally acknowledge, the overt indicators of a drunk about to take flight. Twice the drunk turns to face us while being checked for weapons. Twice he flinches ever so slightly as his booze-soaked mind weighs his chances of successful flight. Twice we don't react as we should.

When the drunk breaks from the tree and starts an alcohol-hampered, zig-zag westbound sprint, it is all I can do not to laugh out loud. *Is this guy serious?* And as I watch the drunk flee, I am taken by surprise when Denny yells out: "Go get him, Mike!" What is even more surprising is that I instinctively take off after the drunk, who now has a block-long head start.

Most people, I believe, think cops like to chase people. On the contrary, nearly every cop I know hates foot pursuits. I am no different. It's not that I am terribly unfit – I'm in better shape than a lot of post-forty guys I grew up with - but toting the weight of an equipment belt, bullet-proof vest and heavy combat-style boots while calling out your direction of travel over the radio during a foot chase is just too damn tiring. Not to mention it often leads to ripped uniform articles and sweaty armpits, particularly on hot summer nights such as this.

The drunk has reached Michigan Avenue now, a hectic four-lane road which runs right smack through Saginaw's Westside business district. I am no more than 10 seconds into this chase when I think about the officer who sent me on this errand. I know damn well Denny is laughing hysterically right now at my expense. I mentally curse his name as I run.

When I hit Michigan Avenue, I cross unchallenged, although as I run I think to myself that I didn't even look for cars. *Boy, would my mom be pissed at that! Or did I look? I can't remember.* Either way, now I'm growing angry.

"Get on the ground, motherfucker!" I scream as I close in on the drunk. I am getting closer as he darts around the exterior wall of a mental health facility, bouncing slightly off the wall as he runs. On the other side of the building I see a patrol car pull up and an officer jump out.

"Police - get down! Get on the ground!" the officer yells. Apparently I'm the only one mad enough to add a "motherfucker" to my commands.

The drunk isn't quite finished yet, though. He turns and doubles back, veering slightly to the north to avoid me. Within seconds he spots a third officer who has joined the chase. Out of options, the drunk goes to his knees, but refuses to get entirely down onto the ground. That changes when I pile on top of him and handcuff him as he spews a string of intoxicated apologies.

On the way back to the scene, the other officers share with me their dislike for chasing idiots. The drunk listens with wandering eyes that cannot focus and a brain that can't fathom why he is now handcuffed, a felony charge waiting on the horizon of his previously clean criminal record.

As we gather statements at the site of the original assault, Central Dispatch throws into the shift the one thing we had been missing for the night. "All units be advised we're getting reports of a triple shooting at The Food Basket." As lights and sirens spark to life and other officers clear our scene to head for more dire surroundings, I look at the apologetic drunk that I now have to baby-sit as he slumps over in the back seat of a nearby patrol car.

Within minutes, the first unit to arrive at the shooting scene calls for crime scene tape. One victim is dead inside a car in the parking lot, and two others are being treated for gunshot wounds.

Inside the jail's booking area moments later, the drunk's apologies turn to disrespect as he wavers between confused confessions of guilt and slurred tirades of mistreatment. Eventually, he asks why I don't like him. I've now had enough.

"Why don't I like you? Because right now I'm stuck here with you while three people just got shot across town. One of them is dead and I'm standing here babysitting your drunken ass."

He chews over my words for a minute until his mind forms a thought: "I hope they all fucking die, man!" he finally screams. His eyes are still unable to maintain focus. I'm sure his brain still hasn't even registered what he just said. I don't respond.

Not long after leaving the jail I learn that all six 3 p.m.-to-3 a.m. shift officers, myself included, have been ordered to work over until we can get the streets under control. A look at my watch shows it's now almost 2 a.m. My night, however, is far from finished.

Long after my normal 3 a.m. departure time has come and gone, amid the arsons and assaults that follow, I think about how quiet my day had been only 12 short hours ago. Then again, quiet – and peace for that matter – never last long when you're a cop.

The Call

The words hit me like a sucker punch in the gut, and I have to steady myself on the kitchen counter.

It is 11 a.m. on a chilly winter day in late December, that time of year when the post-Christmas doldrums leave you with nothing but the long wait for the return of springtime. I had been staring out the window at puffy grey December clouds as I poured a bowl of cereal. When the phone rang, I absent-mindedly picked it up without even checking the caller ID.

"Hello, Michael," said the voice on the other end, the voice of my father.

The call started as most of our phone conversations; my father and I normally talk every week or two. But five minutes into the conversation his voice tone lowers and he begins to ramble briefly about inconsequential topics. I can sense he is stalling. Being a cop, I frequently have to deliver bad news. I know the routine. I know he is trying to decide how to tell me something.

I have learned through my job that when you cannot find the right words, the best course of action is to just keep it simple and get the facts out. Simple and factual, that's the way to go.

"I've got a brain tumor," he says abruptly.

The words linger briefly as my mind tries to digest the information it's just received. For a moment I want to ignore the remark, just pretend I never heard it. I say nothing. Subconsciously I suppose I am hoping he just

116

moves on to a different topic – last night's Red Wings' hockey game maybe – and we'll continue small talking like we always do, devoting no time to serious subjects like sickness, cancer and death. I get my fill of death at work.

"I've been having problems with my eyes for a while and my eye doctor couldn't seem to find the problem," he continues, unaware that I am still trying to asses the validity of his previous statement. "Anyway, he consulted some doctors and I had some tests done and they found a brain tumor. They're going to have to drill a hole in my head and do a biopsy."

I am still stunned and haven't yet responded. This registers with him now.

"They'll be lucky to even find a brain in my head," he says, forcing a slight chuckle to ease me into the conversation.

My father and I never had a normal relationship; time and circumstances dictated that. For a good many years our relationship was strained, even tumultuous. But over the past decade or so we managed to work out our differences – better understand each other's perspectives might be more accurate – and forge a solid, late-life, father-and-son relationship.

My father and mother married in the early 60's, more out of obligation than anything, I suppose. Oh, I am sure they loved each other. But love is sometimes not enough to sustain a young couple barely out of high school. Throw into the mix an unexpected newborn child – my older brother – and you've got a recipe for marital disaster, especially at a time when out-of-wedlock pregnancies were much less acceptable than they are today.

I am sure my birth, which I am told was also unexpected, did nothing to help solve whatever marital problems my parents were experiencing at the time. Without doubt, there are many more untold events, many more shattered dreams and a bevy of silent, trampled-on feelings that make up the path of my parents' love, marriage and subsequent divorce. But I am not privy to the back story of their relationship. For me, the simple fact was this: My parents divorced when I was young and I grew up, like many kids I see on the streets today, not really knowing my father.

It took several years to realize I was different from my peers, but the realizations and my corresponding frustration grew as I aged. None of my friends stood by the curb on Friday nights, suitcase at their side, waiting for their father to pick them up for the weekend, ignoring their mother's pleas to come back inside the house to wait. The anxiety she experienced watching me gaze down the street could have been matched only, I think, by my fear of missing my ride if I was not visible when my father's '72 Pontiac finally pulled into the driveway.

Weekends at my dad's place passed quickly, and never really offered much time with my father anyway. My dad had a new wife and a new family to support. He supplemented his regular paycheck with part-time jobs that kept him busy on the weekends. While I never liked it much, I became accustomed to the fact that time with my father was rare. Quality one-on-one time, the moments where a father provides guidance and direction to a growing boy, was even rarer. Ironically, my life's experiences - or lack thereof - with my father, have proven valuable to me as a police officer. I can now easily relate to the uncountable fatherless and directionless children I encounter every day in the unforgiving streets of urban America.

As I grew, my resentment toward my father also blossomed. Years passed and I went to high school and, later, headed to college to learn about life. As I became back then what I considered a worldly man, I recall consciously thinking that life really wasn't all that hard. And, as I grew confident with the illusion that I had life by the proverbial balls, I found myself less and less understanding of all that had caused my father to become estranged from his family in the first place.

Eventually, the chasm between my father and I grew to the point that other family members begged me to seek a meeting to salvage our relationship. I resisted these promptings and I recall thinking I no longer needed anyone, my father included. I had every reason to hate my father then with the same passion I often hate "the streets" now. I had become the only person I could trust. And, while my anger toward my father eventually dissipated, the feeling that I can trust no one still serves me well, at least while I'm in uniform. Even in personal relationships, I let very few people into my comfort zone, choosing instead to shun potential new friends in lieu of keeping only the old, familiar ones. Some say I'm far too quick to dismiss even a close friend when I feel they've wronged me.

Sitting with my dad at an Irish pub one sunny afternoon we finally agreed that we had both hurt each other, and we decided our relationship was worth rebuilding. I gained a better understanding of the things that drove a confused young man to leave his family. He finally got to hear the pain his decisions wrought upon a young child. We both grew a bit that day.

"When is your surgery; I want to come down?" I ask my father now, speaking for the first time in this new, life-and-death conversation.

He gives me the details of the procedure, but says I don't have to come. "That's not necessary, Michael. I'll be fine."

Eventually, we agree that I will be there when he has his surgery, and we hang up after offering some generic words of mutual support. In truth, I had no idea what to say to him. When I set the phone in its holder, I turn to see my wife quietly watching from the staircase. She asks what is going on. The words will not come, but the tears that so often escape me in the streets flow freely now.

The past few months have produced a litany of challenges for my family. Following my grandmother's death in September, my wife went through a life-saving operation that left her hospitalized and off work for months. While my wife healed, I learned my older brother had developed a chest tumor. And, while his recovery is promising, my step-sister would not be so fortunate. A re-occurrence of cancer has now re-claimed her health and will take her life within weeks of my father's brain tumor announcement. It all crashes down on me now and I sob uncontrollably. For all that I've seen on the streets, I've never felt the unbearable pain that I feel at this moment.

Days later, my father's exploratory surgery goes as scheduled. After the surgery, the doctor breaks the news I have known would come since we spoke on the phone as I stood in my kitchen on that cold December morning. The tumor is large, it is inoperable and it will kill him . . . it's only a matter of when.

"I would say anywhere from one to five years," the surgeon says calmly, as he explains that the location and configuration of the tumor makes an operation far too risky. He speaks flatly. He speaks firmly. He is as disconnected as I know I sound when I tell a mother her young son has been gunned down and will never be coming home. Oddly, I admire his ability to remove himself emotionally and be a clear messenger. He has been down this road before. So have I, but I've never seen it from this side until today.

"We can do some radiation and chemotherapy," he concludes, "but that is only to buy time."

I see my father briefly in his hospital room before I leave. The room is as cold and sterile as I feel at this moment. He jokes that he would love a cold beer. I force a laugh. He has not been told the news and he is still too drugged, I hope, to see what we already know. I've got a bad poker face when it comes to personal matters, so I try not to look him directly in the eye. After about 20 minutes I leave so my father can rest. We part with a limp, cold handshake and a weak hug. His body is too drained to offer much more, but his eyes show nothing but love. My two-hour drive home is a blur which, to this day, I cannot recall.

Days later, my father's treatment has been mapped out. He will undergo an intertwined radiation and chemotherapy regiment to try and slow the growth of the tumor that will eventually take his life. The radiation treatments will be weekly. Eventually, due to my father's worsening condition, we decide he should not drive to the treatments. I tell him I will drive him and he reluctantly agrees, despite a weak argument to the contrary.

Two days before our first trip I call my father to finalize our plans. He is confused. He cannot remember directions from his house to the hospital. He cannot tell me when to pick him up. He is frustrated and scared. So am I.

My usual three-mile run this morning is an emotional odyssey. My thoughts range from anger, to guilt, to frustration, to sadness as I run, mile after mile after mile. But as hard and as fast as my legs move, I cannot escape the reality from which I flee. Toward the last mile or two I shake from fatigue and dehydration, but continue running. Ten miles later I look over my shoulder, but my past, and the present day it has produced, are right there keeping pace.

Finally, the day of my father's appointment arrives. It's a bitter cold February morning and my alarm clock goes off at 4:30 a.m. After a quick shower I load my car, say goodbye to my wife and strike out for a two-hour drive to take my dad to his first radiation treatment.

My father has been a hard-working man all his life. Eventually, he saved enough money to purchase a franchise outlet of a nationally known auto repair chain. The location he purchased was a perennial dog in terms of its regional sales ranking. Within a few short years, however, he had it performing beyond anybody's expectations and he was able to sell off the franchise, and retire to a waterfront home he had purchased some years prior. He had hoped to spend his retirement years boating, fishing and enjoying the growth of his grandchildren. His plans have changed dramatically now.

When I walk into the kitchen of my father's house, his wife says he has had a bad night. He apparently experienced some brain swelling, which has caused noticeable dexterity problems. When he comes into the room, he is shaky and confused. I can see the frustration in his eyes as he tries to talk, but the words come out jumbled.

On the way to the hospital I carry most of the conversation and give him questions that require simple "yes" or "no" answers. He looks at me now with confusion and pleading in his eyes. This is the first time I have ever seen weakness in my father. It is unsettling, but I do my best to mask my uneasiness. I point as we pass a lake where we once skated together all day. This brings a smile to his face and a gleam to his eyes that only memories of a happier time can provide.

Eventually we enter a busy four-lane thoroughfare not far from the hospital. I absent-mindedly ask aloud what street I am supposed to look for. My father, a man who has always prided himself on knowing the quickest and most direct route to anywhere in metropolitan Detroit, answers eagerly: "Get into the left lane and turn left at wet nose," he says. "When you get to wet nose, you gotta make a quick left."

I manage to maintain an even expression, despite my fear of what his mangled words might mean – that his cancer is farther advanced than even the doctors had thought. He realizes immediately that the words he formed in his mind were not the ones his mind sent to his mouth. He looks to the floorboard in fear and embarrassment.

"Don't worry," I tell him. "I've drank beers with you enough times to know what you're trying to say." This joke brings a hearty laugh from both of us as we are able to push back the seriousness of this day, if only for a few seconds.

When we pull into the parking lot, I offer to get my father a wheelchair. As I expect, he refuses. I have to walk close to him, though, because he keeps walking into parked cars, door frames and anything else that resides within 10 feet of his path. Mercifully, our stay at the hospital is short and we are back at his house by 11 a.m.

When I leave for my two-hour drive back to Saginaw, my father says he is going to sleep for a while. We part with a hug and, as I leave, I cannot believe he has aged so much in just a few weeks. I arrive in Saginaw at about 2 p.m. and drive straight to the police station to begin my shift, still trying to shake off the horrors of my day's experience.

During my career I have, from time to time, been engaged in debate by several non-police officers who like to argue that police work is not really a stressful occupation. I don't carry the debate for long these days. There is simply no way of understanding the physical and psychological challenges of urban law enforcement unless you've experienced the job firsthand.

Everybody experiences emotional and physical challenges, and cops certainly do not own the franchise on suffering. As police officers we make our way as best we can through our own personal pain . . . and then we go out and try to calmly and objectively deal with everyone else's. That is the hardest part.

I quietly pack my patrol car just after 3 p.m., distancing myself from my co-workers as I prepare to serve the citizens of this violent community. Then I think about how so many people are willing to simply throw their lives away with drugs and gangs and guns while some – my father is at the top of this list – would give anything for a simple clean bill of health. I try, but I simply cannot make sense of it all. Life's lack of fairness is the thought that stays with me my entire shift.

During my father's struggle with his disease there were highs and there were lows. There were scary moments and there were times of hope. He spent most of his last weeks in bed, his physically ravaged body finally unable to support him. Through the suffering, fear, paralysis and confusion he still managed to smile from time to time.

On a breezy October afternoon, I was able to meet my dad's pastor and take communion with my father as he sat, mostly helpless, in a hospital bed inside his home. These few moments gave me pause to reflect on our relationship and the influence my father has had on my life. My final hours with my dad taught me more about compassion than years of being a cop. I pray these times will help me bring that compassion to the worn urban streets I patrol and the people I serve there.

Wouldn't that be a fine tribute to my father?

Michael S. East

Author's Note: Donald East died quietly early one morning nearly three years after being diagnosed with brain cancer. I was en route to be with him after receiving a phone call that his time was near. I was not with him when he died; he passed away before I was able to make it to his side.

On a brisk and sunny November day in 2008, my father's funeral was held at a small Lutheran church not far from his home. Members of the Saginaw Police Department Honor Guard, attired in white gloves and dress uniforms, stood silent vigil beside my father during his showing. An eight-officer detail escorted my father's casket into and out of his church for his funeral service, and stood in formation in silent salute as his casket was taken to a waiting hearse. Surrounded by my family, and by my police family, I said goodbye to my dad. I have never been more proud of my father, or my profession, than at that moment. I hope my dad feels the same.

The Cop Attitude

The truth is undeniable. I am a changed person since becoming a cop. I have developed The Cop Attitude.

Police officers often are accused of owning a certain disposition. We possess an air of distrust, stiffness and sometimes even cockiness that remains largely misunderstood by the general public. It is an attitude that cannot be fathomed unless you have worn the badge for an extended period of time. It is an attitude that is vital to maintain a certain level of sanity. It is an attitude necessary to survive.

I recall a police training seminars I attended in the late 90s that focused on breaking down what was referred to as the "Us versus Them" attitude. The thought was that cops view the world as "Us" (cops) against "Them" (society). I was told this outlook is detrimental to my success as a police officer. After years on the streets, I have come to the conclusion that this outlook is as necessary as the gun I carry with me each day.

From the moment I put on my uniform at the start of the work day I am different from everyone else. I am scorned for eating my lunch in a public place, as passersby proclaim sarcastically: "I'm glad to see you eating your lunch on my tax dollar." I am admonished by speeding drivers for citing their dangerous driving habits when "there are more serious crimes going on." These are the same people who undoubtedly clamor for more police patrols to stop the speeders near the schools their children attend. I have been told by murderers that I should be out catching child molesters. I have been screamed at by child molesters that I should be out catching murderers. In today's guiltless society, blame is often, and without hesitation, heaped upon the shoulders of law enforcement officers.

On any given day, the media spews forth lead stories and front page headlines calling into question police tactics and practices. An armed man was shot by the police – did they use too much force? A man was restrained with non-lethal force – are the police taser happy? Why did the cops not act faster? Were the police not cautious enough; did they rush in too soon? Police officers are asked to perform their duties and put their lives on the line every day. And every day, the second-guessing continues by those who would never dream of risking their own lives to help a perfect stranger.

And yet, for all the Monday morning quarterbacking, some very obvious questions are very rarely asked: Why do cops get divorced at a higher rate than the general public? Why are cops more prone to alcoholism than those in most other professions? Why is the suicide rate for police officers so much higher than the national average? These questions are too often overlooked for the sake of eye-catching headlines and finger-pointing. As a society, we are constantly searching for answers to crime and violence, yet we rarely devote a thought to the toll taken on those charged with combating the criminals we so fear.

It's a cold pre-Thanksgiving day in mid-November when I pull up in front of a house on the city's west side, responding to a family trouble in progress. An adult woman has called to complain about a problem with her mother. The dispatch call says the woman's mother has taken the woman's welfare benefits card, known in Michigan as a "Bridge Card," and is refusing to give it back.

Another officer and I knock on the front door several times, but nobody answers. After a couple minutes the caller pulls back the curtains of the front window and stares at us in silence. The curtains fall back into place and she is gone. Not a word is said. We eventually leave without ever speaking to her.

Several moments later I am crossing a bridge back to my assigned patrol beat on the east side of town. My trip is cut short, however, as I am sent back to the same house. The woman has called again asking for police assistance with the same problem. No explanation is given for why she refused to talk to us only moments ago.

Arriving at the same house, I find myself knocking on the same door again. This time both the mother, a stern-looking woman in her fifties, and her twenty-something daughter come out onto the porch. The mother informs us that her daughter is hooked on crack cocaine. *There's a shock* says a sarcastic voice in my head. She says the woman has been trading her "Bridge Card" credits for drugs. The daughter is jumpy, rude and twitches uncontrollably. Her drug abuse is apparent.

"All I wanna do is get my 'Bridge Card' and take my kids to get some outfits," she proclaims, insisting also that she has no drug problem. "I can drop for you right now. All you'll find is marijuana, but everybody does that."

The mother is tired of arguing, says she doesn't have her daughter's "Bridge Card," walks inside and shuts and locks the front door. The daughter is incensed and turns her venom toward me now. She wants me to kick in the door and find her welfare card. I tell her I cannot.

I have never met this woman before, but I can see in her eyes what is coming - she is going to make her problems my problems. Like so many people I deal with, she wants the police to be the quick fix to the life of misery she has built for herself. Those addicted souls which form the soundtrack to nearly every one of my work days have a knack for pointing the finger of blame at anybody but themselves.

"What the fuck good are you then if you don't do your fucking job!" she screams.

I remain calm – this is no simple task – as I inform the woman that I cannot violate her mother's rights by arbitrarily kicking in her front door. *I find it funny how some people are not concerned about the police protecting people's rights if it's someone else's rights that are in question.* I mentally brace for her verbal onslaught.

"You can't violate her rights? What the fuck good are you then?" she continues, turning to my partner now. "You're just a smartass white cop, aren't you? You hate black people!"

"You and your mother are both black," says my partner, pointing out the lack of logic in the woman's statement. Her response is quick and to the point: "I hate you motherfucking police!" Our conversation ends here. The best thing we can do at this point is exactly what we do - walk away.

This call is nothing special. It is, in fact, a replica of dozens of similar calls I respond to every week where I am held to blame for everything that is going wrong in the lives of people I have never met. My job is a constant battle to balance humanity, humility and enough Cop Attitude to not get killed.

It's just after midnight on a warm night in early June. I am on routine patrol, but when two other officers are dispatched to a report of a man down on the sidewalk, I disregard one of the officers as I am only two blocks away. I find the man, and another intoxicated companion, lying in the front yard of an abandoned house about five feet from the sidewalk. Less than a block away booze-buying customers flow in and out of a liquor store, a store jokingly referred to by cops as the *Stop-And-Rob.*

When I approach the two men, one is completely unconscious. The other teeters on the brink of incoherency. I summon an ambulance to transport the two to a local hospital to dry out. And, as the lesser of the two drunks babbles aloud and tries to stagger to his feet, I take notice of what a beautiful night it is. Through the trees, the sky is alive with stars, and the warm summer air pushes a slight breeze against my face.

I am pulled back to reality as Lesser of Drunks finally gets to his feet. "Man, I just wanna go home. Let me get him up and we'll just go home," he says, nodding his head toward the man who still lies passed out in the lawn.

"Just sit down. I'm gonna have an ambulance come by and check you guys out and make sure you're ok."

The man gets fidgety now. He struggles to stay on his feet as he reaches clumsily toward his pockets. He continues to avoid my requests for him to sit down. When my backup officer pulls up to the scene via the sidewalk, Lesser of Drunks really gets squirrelly.

"Man, now you're making me nervous. Get over here," I tell him.

My backup officer walks up just as I ask the man if he has anything illegal on him. He remains quiet. When I pat him down he resists as much as a nearly comatose drunk can. He is carrying a fully loaded pistol in his right pocket. When I pull it out, he lets out a drunken sigh not nearly as loud as the moan in my subconscious at the exact same moment.

"That's a pretty nice gun," says the other cop at the scene as I handcuff Lesser of Drunks. He is making a point to me, but there is really no need. I am mentally kicking my own ass right now.

Like other cops, sometimes I lose focus and take a call too lightly. Sometimes I take time to enjoy the scenery while forgetting I am wearing a uniform. Sometimes I forget who the bad guy is. In my world *everybody* is the bad guy.

It's mid afternoon and the Central Dispatch alert tone disrupts afternoon roll call like a dentist's drill striking raw nerve. An out-and-out gunfight on the city's near west side sends us scrambling for equipment.

For three minutes, during my jog to my patrol car and 100-miles-per-hour drive to the venue, gunfire rages in the streets of this once quiet neighborhood. It is mid-afternoon and schools are just letting children out for the day. I can envision the worst as reports come in over the radio every 10 or 15 seconds. Central Dispatch advises there are two victims down in the street. Several vehicle descriptions are also given, although it is hard to discern if they are involved in the shooting, or they are innocent bystanders fleeing for safety.

When I arrive at scene, mayhem has taken over the block. Officers from neighboring jurisdictions, having been alerted to the incident, have arrived to assist the dozen or so city officers already here. Citizens, too short on common sense to stay in their houses, run here and there and have to be escorted from the scene while we struggle to locate both the victims and the suspects.

Not knowing who was firing the shots, officers crouch and duck for cover as we swarm the neighborhood. After a few minutes, the victims are accounted for and are secured. The suspects are supposedly holed-up inside a nearby house. Another officer and I quickly secure the rear of the house and we remain at this post for a couple hours, guns trained on the back doors and windows. Eventually, the Emergency Services Team (EST) arrives, the house is entered and a suspect is taken into custody. I am later told the shootings stemmed from a drug deal gone awry.

This incident catches more media attention than most during the year - a year when Saginaw will eventually see 26 homicides and about 140 actual shootings. The numbers are staggering for a city of less than 60,000 people, and give Saginaw a higher violent crime rate per capita than many larger cities with far worse reputations. They are not exactly the type of numbers one would include in a Chamber of Commerce brochure.

Later in the night, after the bodies have been picked up, the bad guys have been locked up and my work shift has ended, I read the day's edition of the local paper. In the Editorial section, a city resident has written a letter to the editor regarding local law enforcement. His opinion: Saginaw has too many police officers.

Us versus them?

You bet.

Addictions

It's 3:30 on a brisk March afternoon. My day has just started and I am driving eastbound on Lapeer Street. Like an agitated race horse shuffling nervously at the starting gate, I await my first radio call of the day. I pass two 12-year-old girls walking down the street. We make eye contact. There is no smile. There is no wave. "Man, fuck the po-lice!" screams one of the girls. The greeting is not unexpected and I drive on without acknowledging the slight.

I am directed moments later by Central Dispatch to a house several blocks away. I am advised there is a disorderly woman at the home and the homeowner cannot get her to leave. When I arrive, a thin, scraggly blonde woman runs from the driveway into the back door of the house and disappears. An equally thin man, who looks like he's in his 50s, comes outside with pleading eyes and a shaky voice: "Man, you gotta get that crazy bitch outta my house . . . Pleeeeeeease."

The man looks old beyond his years and it's hard to tell his exact age. Too much hard living has taken its toll on his body and his mind. He tells me he had invited the woman over the night before for a drug party. Now all the drugs are gone and she won't leave his house. These are the people I have sworn to serve and protect.

I am annoyed and unenthused when I go inside with a backup officer to clean up the leftovers of last night's crack binge. The woman is standing in the kitchen now and skitters into a bathroom at the sight of us. Despite our orders, she refuses to come out. Eventually, we force open the bathroom door and find the woman crouched in a corner like a caged animal. She has that distant look in her eyes that I see often on the faces of the legions of drug-crazed zombies that roam the streets of Saginaw, night and day. It is the look of sheer insanity.

"Man, watch out. That bitch is crazy!" the man exclaims as he steps inside the back door.

Suddenly, the woman dashes toward us. The other officer and I grab onto her and try to handcuff her. She is wiry and she is wired. Her thin features and surprising cocaine-induced strength make her hard to hold onto. She fights and she kicks and she claws, the open sores on her arms passing within inches of my face as we tussle. I've got her in a bear hug now, but she kicks her feet up and begins walking up the wall. Finally, we all fall backward and tumble onto the floor where we get the woman handcuffed.

She screams relentlessly. Her breath smells like old cheese, rotting teeth and decaying flesh.

Outside, the woman fights even more as we try to stuff her into a patrol car. When my partner goes to the other side of the car to pull the woman through into the back seat, the crack addict straddles my right leg like she's riding a horse. She mounts her feet in the doorframe of the car and kicks herself away from it. Then I feel the warmth on my pant leg. She is urinating on me. I am fuming now. I throw the woman to the ground and, with the assistance of two other officers who have arrived, finally force her into my patrol car to await an ambulance. She is far too high to go to jail and will need to go to the hospital for treatment instead.

Inside the car, the woman screams incessantly as the foamy spittle from her dried mouth flings against the car window. Her words are incoherent. Her eyes are sunken into deep, dark ruts. Her face is a picture of crazed madness. I wonder for a moment how she got to such a place in her life.

The backgrounds of drug addicts used to be of more interest to me. There are literally hundreds, quite possibly thousands, of stories of personal ruination on the streets of

Saginaw. They are not hard to find, those persons with gaunt-looking faces, wearing disheveled clothes, driving beat-up, filthy cars. They can be located at any given moment, in the drug neighborhoods, stopped in the middle of the road with groups of young men reaching into their car windows completing another don't-blink-or-you'll-miss-it dope deal.

The script repeats itself every time a cop car turns the corner and interrupts the sale: The dealers quickly disappear into nearby backyards, cyclone fences rattling as they flee for safety. The buyer drives off in a controlled hurriedness, careful to use turn signals at every corner in hopes of not getting pulled over. Their excuse for being 15 miles from home, stopped in the middle of the roadway with dope dealers hanging from their car, usually involves being lost, trying to find an unnamed restaurant, or looking for the home of "a friend," the name of whom has suddenly escaped them.

Most drug addicts deny their actions to the bitter end. When a search of their car – that disgusting, trash-infested, four-wheeled monstrosity that provides transportation to their next high – yields a rock or two, or a crack pipe, they often "have no idea how that got in there." Sometimes the denials are so strong, I think they convince themselves they are not actually addicted. However, a few, a very slim few, beaten down by the miserable lives they lead, speak with a certain amount of candor and offer an unobstructed view into their world of addiction.

Several years ago, I pulled over a man in his late 50s, my attention being drawn to him as he cruised all the drug hotspots at dope-buyer speed, awaiting the arrival of a salesman, any salesman, to feed his need. The man's story was quite unsettling. A retired automotive industry executive living on a more-than-generous pension, he was now reduced to driving a 10-year-old, rusting, rattling compact car which he could not afford to insure. His wife and children had left him. He had no place of residence, save for a small cabin "up north." The man looked physically, mentally, and emotionally to be two steps from death's door. His only

Michael S. East

source of excitement now, he confessed, was finding drugs and a prostitute who could entertain him until the month's pension check ran out.

The stories vary somewhat, but carry the common theme of addiction. They bore me now. Like a once interesting movie seen too many times, the storyline has gone flat. Urban America is overflowing with persons imprisoned by drugs. By night they wander the streets, looking for their next fix. By day, they flag down cops or arrive at police stations with stories of being carjacked, or robbed. The stories eventually break down into the truth: they traded their car for a couple rocks of crack cocaine. These are the cars that usually end up being used in drive-by shootings and homicides.

Oddly, some police officers have a common bond with the dope fiends with which we deal. Most cops I know are also addicted - hung up on that high, that adrenaline rush, which permeates their lives through their chosen profession. If the high of crack cocaine is anything like the rush of driving pedal-to-the-floor to a gunfight, the attraction is not all that hard to understand. The only difference is that most cops manage to harness the madness, and keep the beast in check.

To some cops, however, the job simply bridges the gap from adrenaline rush to other habits. I know police officers who have heard the beast knock on the door one too many times . . . and they answered it. They thought they knew the beast well enough to contain it. But they could not, and eventually they found themselves caught up on the wrong side of the addiction game.

Most commonly, cops seem to turn to alcohol to sup-plement their rush, or to shave the sharp edges from a harsh day on the streets. It is well known that cops suffer from a high rate of alcoholism. I have known many police officers who were - and some who still are - alcoholics. I have known others who had drug addictions. Along with suicide and infidelity, drug/alcohol abuse combines to form that dangerous trinity which, to one extent or another, causes the demise of many of my kind.

There are many times, after an unusually violent or stressful shift, I come home and want nothing more than two or three bottles of beer to settle myself and fight off the work-related dreams that often seep into my sleep. And while I realize seeking refuge from stress in a bottle of beer is not healthy, it is a far cry from my youthful cop days when shift's end was often celebrated with co-workers in a three-hour trip to the local tavern to re-tell the day's stories. At least this is how I rationalize my behavior now during those times I feel the need to numb myself from a day on the streets.

As I watch a crack-crazed woman get strapped to a stretcher and hauled off to a hospital for treatment that will surely not help her, I think for a moment that it is a finer line than most would like to admit that separates the good guys from the bad.

5:13 a.m.

It's a dark night as I chase him through a residential area. He just fired a shot at me and, by God, I'm not letting this guy get away. I didn't get a look at his face, this man clad in all black clothing, but I'm only steps behind. Identification will come after I catch this guy and beat the living shit out of him.

As we change direction and round a corner, the gap between us widens. He's not running any faster and my pace has not slowed, but he's pulling away from me now with ease. I'm far from being the best-conditioned cop on the streets, but a daily weights and running routine dictates that I should be able to catch this guy.

I briefly re-holster my gun as I reach for my radio to call out the foot chase. The awkward process of simultaneously running and yelling out directions goes smoothly. But my words go unanswered. The dispatcher fails to repeat my situation to other officers. No co-workers hurriedly exclaim that they're en route to back me up. There is only silence.

As we round the next corner, I can barely see my shadowy assailant. We have run into woods now. *What happened to the houses? Where the hell are we?* I have no backup and now I don't even know where I am. The chase continues even though I no longer can see him. I look to my left and to my right. *Who's the prey now?*

Finally I stop the chase, look around, bend over and take a few deep breaths. I curse aloud my incompetence. He is long gone. This guy – *who the hell was he?* – raised a gun

136

and fired a single shot at me. And now he's escaped. *Where am I again?*

I ponder my whereabouts only for a moment before being distracted by movement to my right. From behind a tree my assailant appears again, gun raised, walking ever-so-slowly toward me. *Is this guy fucking crazy?*

Instinct takes over and my gun is drawn and leveled at his head in a micro-second. I spew forth the usual commands for him to drop the gun. God forbid you defend your own life without giving an armed suspect a few extra seconds to kill you by first yelling for him to "drop the fucking gun!"

"Officer East, isn't it true that you gave this poor individual only three commands to drop his weapon before you ruthlessly and mercilessly gunned him down in cold blood?" the suspect's attorney would surely bellow in court. "And isn't it true that had you shown the humanity to issue five verbal warnings and fired a warning shot, this man's precious life – he was planning on going back to school and recently found God, you know – might have been spared from your brazen lack of respect for human life?"

My verbal warnings prove pointless. The man, gun extended, continues his menacing walk toward me. There is nothing else I can do. My mind does a quick flip through my alternatives and there is only one which is plausible. I steady my gun hand and squeeze twice on the trigger as I simultaneously give one more drop-the-gun command.

There is now only silence; silence and nothing more.

No ear-ringing gunshots. No muzzle flash. No suspect screaming in agony. My gun has misfired, leaving my ears with nothing more to process than two tiny *clicks* as I now await my own fate.

The man smiles, walks within mere feet and steadies his gun at my head as I await an ending to my cop story; an ending I now realize was inevitable from Day One of the police academy. I close my eyes and prepare for death.

I am choking slightly as I awake from this dream, and it takes several seconds to realize the familiarity of my surroundings. It used to take longer, but the more times I return – I have frequent flyer tickets to this nightmare which my mind cashes in a half-dozen times per year – the quicker I am able to re-acclimate myself to reality.

I look now past my still-sleeping wife toward the bright red numbers on the alarm clock. It's 5:13 a.m.

The dreams themselves differ only slightly, but then end result – failure – always resonates. Sometimes I never catch up to the bad guy at all. Sometimes we have a gun fight and every one of my steadily placed rounds misses. Every now and then, like tonight, my gun misfires at a critical point. Occasionally during the shootout the bullets simply drop from the barrel of my 40-calibur Glock handgun straight to the ground. Always the suspect remains faceless. Always he gets away.

Sometimes there is no gunman. Sometimes there is only the face of a young girl named Karen, a girl pleading for my help, an innocent girl begging for me to save her. Always I fail her. Sometimes there is a young boy named Mick, a sad-faced child wallowing in the abusive nightmare which is his life. He stares at me in silence. There are no tears - that well ran dry long ago. There are only pain-filled eyes seeking understanding and compassion. I try but can provide neither, and he turns and walks away in silence.

Over the years I have heard other cops confess simi-lar dreams, so I assume I'm not the only one who visits this land of nightmare failures on a regular basis. I just never run into another cop there. I am sure a good psychologist would have a field day with these recurring dreams. But I am not much for having my mind picked apart by a stranger.

Once during my lifetime I've visited a psychologist and the experience was quite unimpressive, although the circumstances dictated only brief interaction between me and the actual mind mechanic. The majority of my experience involved taking a test to evaluate, I would imagine, my mental stability. I wonder if the test results would have changed from that day to this.

It was 1994, and prior to being selected for employment with the Saginaw Police Department, I was required to pass a psychological exam, one of those precautions police departments have to take to ensure they hire the law-abiding crazy people as opposed to the criminal lunatics.

I arrived the day of my test at a rather mundane-looking brick building which sat alongside a cornfield several miles north of the city limits. The building looked like an actual house, but the even-toned, no-nonsense dispositions of the people inside gave the place a cold, unfriendly feel.

My several-hundred-question multiple choice test was taken inside a stuffy little room with blandly paneled walls. The room was furnished with a desk and a single chair. The only wall décor was a large mirror, which I am quite sure was of the two-way monitoring type that allowed observation of the test-takers.

Completing the test was more time-consuming than anything and I was not too concerned about the questions. "Don't try to beat this test," I was told by the officer conducting my background investigation. "Just provide honest answers or you might come out sounding nuts." Good advice.

My only odd experience during test-taking time was when a black ant came crawling out from underneath the mirror frame, down the wall and onto the desk where I was slowly putting my Number 2 pencil through the paces. I raised my hand slightly to complete my immediate reaction of smashing ant guts onto the table. But then I remembered the previous test question revolved around finding a wounded animal and asking if I would take the time to help it. *This ant is a plant by the shrink!* my tired mind had rationalized on that day. So I gently brushed the ant off the desk with one hand into the other and set it on the floor. In the observation room I was sure I was being graded highly in the category of humanitarianism. "He spared the ant; this is a good prospect," my observers on the opposite side of the two-way mirror were surely saying. Looking back now I think the brick house near the cornfield simply had an infestation problem.

My evaluation meeting with a psychologist, a tall, thin man with graying hair, a too-polite demeanor and probing eyes, went smoothly. We talked for only about 10 minutes and he must have declared me sane. Fifteen years have passed since that exam and I think now the desired result of that meeting – my being hired to police these hopeless streets – should have been cause enough for an insanity ruling then and there.

Even as I make my way through the life of a cop and I cope with the fears, frustrations and anxieties inherent to the job, I have yet to feel the need to seek professional help to figure out the dark spots in my mind. I have, I believe, figured them out on my own.

My mind re-visits these nightmare places as a way to deal with my failures, both as a cop and as a person. These are the mental timeshares of which my mind has taken ownership. I visit them because I failed to save the life of Karen King, whose innocent face still plagues my thoughts and dreams. I visit them because my words were not enough to stop a young teen from walking out the door of the police department and into a life of nothingness. I visit them because a kid named Mick reached out for a helping hand that never came.

Failure is an inevitable part of being a cop and it's the one part you cannot walk away from. The failures that I experience now – they pile up every day, every week and every year - will, I fear, stay with me long after the job is over.

Sometimes I feel I will never totally escape being a cop.

Protect and Serve

I've come to learn over the years that, in law enforcement, there is a large gap between expectations and reality. When I joined the fraternity of police officers, I was much more naïve than I realized. I had high expectations: I was going to save lives, right the wrongs and be the strong voice of reason. It didn't take long to learn the harsh realities: Lives sometimes go unsaved, the wrongs often never get righted, and the voice of reason usually goes unheard against the gunfire, screams and insanity of the streets.

But that's not even the worst of it. Beyond the hopelessness of the bad guys and the bodies and the blood, is something even more disturbing. The one thing I may never learn to cope with is the ungratefulness of a public that often finds only fault in the actions of those who try to keep peace in the streets.

It's a bright and sunny October day as I sit in my patrol car talking to another officer. Radio traffic has been light for the first hour of my shift and we talk about a variety of non-cop topics: college football, the turning leaves of autumn, and maybe taking a weekend road trip up north before the weather becomes too cold. For a few blissful moments we converse like normal people, and talk about normal things. No mention of bad guys or bullets or guns. That should have been my first clue that things were about to go to shit.

When the call goes out for a teen walking through a west side neighborhood toting a gun, my ears immediately perk up. The suspect description is very detailed, and that usually is a good indication that the call isn't just a prank set up to watch the cops running around chasing their tails. Neither myself nor the officer I am talking to are dispatched to the call, but without a word we instinctively put our cars in gear and start for the location to assist the three west side units that are already responding.

It takes less than a minute for the first unit, a K-9 officer, to arrive on scene and only seconds for him to call out that he's in a foot chase. The suspect is running westbound. I light up my overheads and hit the siren as I race toward the Holland Street Bridge, the tires of my patrol car screeching wildly as I pilot through the curves of the bridge's approach.

Radio traffic indicates the suspect is still running westbound as I carefully jog my way through a couple busy intersections. About 10 other police cars are en route to the call now, and I am careful to avoid any unwanted meetings in the crossings I am trying to navigate. I arrive just as an officer at scene announces the suspect is holed up somewhere within a one-block area.

Containment is important when it comes to chasing bad guys on foot. If you cannot catch them within the first couple blocks, it's always good to at least trap them within the confines of a particular area. By this time, officers are now set up on the four corners of the block where the suspect is hiding. Any attempts by the bad guy at getting out of this perimeter will result in immediate detection. The only thing left to do now is send officers into the block to check the hiding spots – inside garages and sheds, underneath cars, and in thickets of bushes – and flush out the perpetrator. The only problem here is that this guy is armed.

I park my patrol car on the street that forms the northern boundary of our perimeter. When I get out, my gun is out at my side and I am focused on the potential danger zones. There is a house to my right and a house to my left.

Straight ahead is a white metal shed, the door of which faces away from me. I will start there. Bad guys love to take refuge in open buildings.

As I make my way toward the shed, covering corners with my handgun to ward off unwanted surprises, I become aware of the eyes of the people in the neighborhood. People have started coming out of their houses now, curious why so many cops are walking their neighborhood with guns drawn. Some stand on porches and watch as their children run up within feet of armed police officers looking for an armed suspect. *Why don't these people go inside their houses?* I have no time for them now. *Stay focused. Stay focused.* I have to concentrate on the task at hand – the teen with the gun.

I clear the shed. Its door is padlocked from the out-side. A privacy fence separates my current location from the next yard. I climb up and peer over quickly, hoping not to get my face shot off. The yard is barren and offers no hiding spots. The bad guy is not there. I move eastbound now, gun at the ready as I clear corners of houses. Still, people mill about across the street. *Why don't these people go inside?* I can feel eyes upon me, and I feel more like an attraction at the local zoo than a cop trying to protect the public. *Focus. There's an armed kid out here. Stay focused.*

I am two houses into the block now and heading south. There are a couple cars in driveways, but nobody lurks beneath them. Radio chatter fills my head, piping into my ears from the mic perched upon my left shoulder. My heart beats quickly in my chest. Another officer walks from behind the next house. He was the guy I was discussing fall road trips with only 10 minutes ago. We make eye contact and he nods to the south. We continue on toward the next house, a single story white structure. I recall being here two weeks ago for a large neighborhood fight.

We walk slowly up the driveway and check under an older car. Nothing. Nobody comes out of either house. They are either smart enough to stay inside or they are not home. Either way, these are the people I appreciate the most at this very moment – the people who are not distracting me. The end of the driveway offers access into two back yards, one to the right and one to the left. I go left. Junk and kid's toys litter the yard. I can hear children screaming in the distance. Curious people are out walking the sidewalks nearby. *Focus. Keep focused.* To my left is a small space between the house and another fence. *Great spot to hide.* I cut the corner, handgun extended. Nobody.

In the next yard the officer I am working with is busy also trying to not get killed. He clears a couple points of interest, but no bad guy is found. I go toward the back yard of the house he is behind. A rickety wood-and-wire fence runs the width of the backyard, separating it from the back yard of the house behind it. The fence leans precariously. When I tug on it, two sections of the fence immediately part, offering enough space for me to squeeze through. In yards nearby other officers mirror our task while searching different landscapes.

When I breech the next yard, my attention is immediately drawn to a large crumbling garage to my left. It's a white wooden structure with peeling paint and two wide doors which both face to the north. He's in there and I can feel it. I get the attention of the other officer and nod toward the garage.

"Hey, guys, who ya lookin' for?" comes a voice from behind a nearby fence.

I divide my attention now between the spot where I know an armed gunman lurks and the voice that has popped up behind me.

A man is quizzing us from behind a nearby fence. I am annoyed by the distraction. The other officer who accompanies me is more patient, however, and engages the man briefly. "We're looking for a teenage kid who came running through here. He's supposed to have a gun."

The man nods toward the garage where I am trying to focus most of my attention. "He's in there," the man whispers. *No shit,* I think to myself as I walk quietly toward the larger of the building's two doors.

My partner is trying to get away from the helpful citizen as I come within a couple feet of the garage. The interior of the building is dark. Gun extended in one hand, I shine a flashlight inside. There is nothing visible but dirt and discarded junk.

Focus. Be careful, whispers my inner voice. *You know he's in here.* I enter the garage, sweeping my gun and flashlight immediately to the right. There, in the darkness, my light illuminates the teen. He's trying to push himself flush against the wall. He's pushing so hard he appears to be trying to become *part* of the wall itself. He's sweating and he's jumpy. His eyes tell me he's trying in vein to wish himself into another time and place far from here. His left hand is visible. His right hand is not.

My gun draws toward him instinctively. "Get your fucking hands up now, or I'll shoot your ass!" His compliance is far too slow and calculated. I still cannot see his right hand. *Watch for a gun! Watch for a gun!* "Show your fucking hands!" I scream as the other officer runs inside the second door.

The teen goes to the ground slowly now, but still will not show his right hand. I give him a firm boot to the back, pushing him to the ground where at least he cannot get off a shot. Our yelling draws a couple more officers to our location.

The teen is lying on the ground now with his hands underneath him. "Get your fucking hands behind your back!" The struggle is brief, but unsettling. We finally pull the kid's hands from underneath him and get him handcuffed. There is no gun.

I am sweating profusely now. My once clean uniform – *Why does it always have to be a clean uniform?* – is covered in dirt. "Do you have a gun?" I yell as I pull the teenager from the ground.

"Naw. I dropped it when that other cop was chasing me."

When we emerge from the garage with the teen in tow I am glad for the happy ending. We come out from

145

behind the house to back track the original foot chase and recover the dropped gun. A bad guy is in custody. Nobody got shot. Nobody got hurt. I feel good about myself now. The moment is brief.

"Thanks, officer, for putting your gun away. There are kids out here, you know." The sarcastic comment comes from a man standing on his front porch a couple houses from where the teen was apprehended.

I am livid. "Excuse me for protecting myself when I'm looking for somebody with a gun." I am sweating and my heart is pounding. It's all I can muster at the moment.

A block away, the teen directs us to the sawed-off shotgun he dropped while being chased. We walk the kid to a police cruiser and secure him in the back seat. About 30 or 40 people mill about on the nearby street and sidewalk. Most of them are kids. A few are parents, at least in the dictionary sense of the word. *Where do all these people come from?*

"Man, look at all you polices," an anonymous voice declares from the crowd.

"He didn't even do nothing," says another.

When the gun is secured, I begin a two-block walk back to my patrol car. I make sure my path leads past the house of the man who had scolded me moments ago. I am calmer now. Maybe he is too. I think it might be a good opportunity to mend a fence with an unhappy citizen. I am wrong.

When I spot the man in his back yard, I immediately approach him.

"Did you have something you wanted to talk to me about?" I ask.

He goes on to tell me how I was wrong to have my gun out while searching his neighborhood. He tells me there are kids in the street and they could have been hurt. I try to explain my need to protect myself when looking for an armed criminal.

"Did you even find a gun? I heard the guy didn't even have a gun. I heard all he did was steal a car," the man says in a cocky tone.

146

"Well, you need to check your information. He did have a gun, and that's why we were trying to catch him in the first place," I respond. My patience is running dangerously thin by this point.

The man is unimpressed. "There are kids out here and you're running around with your gun out. Somebody could have been hurt."

I engage the man about the dangers of police work and staying focused in the face of so many distractions. "I'm a trained police officer. I'm not going to go looking for an armed guy without my gun out. I know when to have my gun out and when not to and, trust me, when I'm looking for somebody with a gun, I'm going to protect myself."

The conversation goes back and forth for a moment or two. Then he says something to which I almost cannot respond. "You know, there are kids out here. You could have said 'Sir, we're looking for a man with a gun. Maybe you should take your children and your family inside.'"

My answer is short and impolite. "I simply don't have time to tell everybody to go inside their houses when I'm trying to concentrate on not getting killed. And let me tell you something, if you need me to tell you to take your kids inside the house when you see a bunch of cops with their guns out searching your neighborhood, then you're a fucking idiot."

As I walk away, both my head and my hands are shaking; I regret the harshness of my words, but there's no taking them back now. Polite or not, I told the man the truth. Maybe it will give him a better understanding of my perspective. More likely, it will not.

The rest of my shift turns out to be as lousy as the first couple hours. Tomorrow I am scheduled to begin a week-long school to become re-certified as a Field Training Officer. The certification will allow me to again train newly hired officers and prepare them to become good street cops.

How can I prepare anybody for a day like this?

A Good Day

It is Sunday, the last of three consecutive 12-hour work days. We had been running short-handed the past couple days and the weekend has been brutally busy. I am looking forward to 3 a.m. and putting this long stretch behind me. But this weekend will refuse to die quietly.

Shortly after 3 p.m. with the workday only moments old, my first call comes over the air – a shooting. The seeds of this call, Saginaw County Central Dispatch advises, had been planted as a report of disorderly persons arguing only moments ago. It quickly blossomed into a much more serious situation.

I am about 15 blocks away from the venue when the call goes out, and I arrive about a minute later, cutting my siren before turning the corner onto the block where the shooting has been reported. People are milling about on both sides of the street and they pay little attention as my patrol car races down the block. There is no hysterical crowd. There is no blood. There is nothing. *Ambush* I think to myself. There have been recent reports that area gang members are plotting to ambush a cop. I do not plan to be the victim.

Backup is still a couple minutes away as I survey the scene from my patrol car. The hairs on the back of my neck are bristling. Central Dispatch holds radio traffic. The quiet is eerie. Up ahead, a man leans against a car parked at the curb. Behind me eight or 10 adult males now watch my every move. Across the street a group of people of all ages sits calmly on their front porch.

Cautiously, I exit my patrol car about 50 feet from the small house where the shooting had been reported. Nobody makes a move. Nobody says a word. There are only probing eyes and silence, a distinctly purposeful quiet that keeps me on edge. Finally, I look toward the man leaning against the car. "Did somebody get shot over here?"

"Yeah, me," he answers matter-of-factly. He takes a step toward me and I can see now he is limping from a bullet wound to the leg.

"Come over here behind this car," I tell him.

"I can't walk, man," he retorts.

"Yes you can. Come over here," I order him. I am way too exposed and I need to use my car for at least some form of cover. "What happened?"

The man limps behind the car to me, then turns and points toward the small house. "That motherfucker shot me."

As the words are leaving his mouth, a man calmly walks onto the front porch and stares at the two of us. "That guy shot you?" I ask, pointing toward the man on the porch.

"Yeah, he just shot me in the leg."

I quickly un-holster my sidearm and order the man off the porch. He does not say a word as he walks slowly toward me, obeying every command. Down the sidewalk the loitering group watches in silence. The man places his hands behind his back, as ordered, and I handcuff him without incident as two patrol cars now race up the road.

Eventually, I am told the shooting was the result of an argument between the two men, although the suspect insists the victim shot himself. Within 20 minutes, the suspect is en route to jail, an ambulance is carting the victim to a local hospital and I have a lengthy report to write.

Prior to reaching the police station another officer announces he has tracked down a stolen car on the city's south side. They are traveling northbound on S. Washington Avenue now. The suspect is refusing to stop. I activate the overheads and siren on my patrol car and race down

Washington Avenue from the north to head off the chase. I arrive moments later just in time to help take three suspects into custody. They had tried to bail out of the car, but were quickly caught by pursuing officers.

After some investigating we find the car was not stolen at all; it was traded for crack cocaine the previous night. Still the driver is arrested and lodged for fleeing and eluding. The two passengers are checked for warrants and released. After half an hour the car's owner arrives to pick up his vehicle. Seven hours from now he will call to again report his car stolen after again trading it to feed his drug habit. For now, though, he has his car back.

An hour later I have completed the previous shooting report and I am clearing up a few stale calls for service. I see there is a felonious assault report waiting at an east side hospital. I volunteer for the call, mostly because it will give me a half-hour break from the road.

At the hospital, the attending nurse relates the details of the assault I am here to document. The victim, it seems, had become involved in a dispute with the suspect after the victim refused to get high with the other man. The suspect took a baseball bat to the man's skull, causing some serious injuries. When the man comes back from getting x-rays, he relates a similar version of the same story. His head is swollen and a large laceration behind his left ear is still bleeding. Before leaving I consult the attending physician and she tells me exactly what I do not want to hear: The man has bleeding on the brain and they cannot be sure if he will live.

I know now this will be no short break from road duties. This information sets into motion a consultation with the shift commander and his subsequent conversation with the weekend detective supervisor. I also round up a road sergeant to get photos of the man's injuries. We then locate the scene where the assault occurred and get numerous photographs of the blood splattered apartment. Finally, an unsuccessful search for the suspect begins. The entire call takes about four hours to complete and I am mentally exhausted when I save my report on a computer at police headquarters.

I am ready for my night to be done. I am ready for this long weekend to be finished. But neither is ready to end. Not by a long shot.

It's closing in on 10 p.m. when I am dispatched to a breaking and entering alarm on the city's north side. Simultaneously, two other patrol cars are responding to a shooting a couple miles from my current location. The shooting sounds minor and two additional cars have also volunteered to respond, so I continue on to my alarm.

Then all hell breaks loose.

Numerous calls come in from the neighborhood of the shooting. There are reports of a home invasion and people being held hostage in a basement. Further calls state a man is chasing a woman through the blocks with a knife, trying to kill her. I divert to the more pressing call now to assist other officers. I am tired. Tired of the day's violence. Tired of the day's lawlessness. Tired of the day's bloodshed. But it's not over quite yet.

With each report given by Central Dispatch, the situation continues to grow direr, and it becomes clear a woman is in danger of being killed. I am a half mile away from the scene when somebody reports seeing a man chasing a woman near an abandoned restaurant on E. Genesee Avenue. When I arrive two other patrol cars are leaving the empty parking lot after finding nobody.

In a stroke of luck I wish I had possessed the night of Karen King's murder, some people walking nearby tell officers a man just dragged a woman into a wooded area on the north side of an auto plant not a block from where I am now. I look to my left. There is a wide swath of knee-high grass extending for about 50 yards. It tapers off into thicker, higher grass with woods beyond and woods to the north. To the south a large fence marks the edge of the auto plant property.

When I jump the curb with my patrol car it immediately becomes bogged down in soft, muddy ruts. *He's going to kill her*. I spotlight ahead and see nobody. *You've got to find her*. I punch the accelerator and get minimal response from my car. *Come on, where are they? Where are they?* I sweep the spotlight right, then left. My car struggles to move forward. *Come on, keep going!* Then I see her. The woman is in a white nightgown, sobbing uncontrollably. Next to her, a large-framed man is holding her down by her shoulders.

"Get the fuck up and show your hands . . . ma'am, stay where you are!" I scream, dividing my attention between suspect and victim. I'm in front of my patrol car, my Glock 40-calibur sighted on the man's head. *When did I get out of the car?* The man looks blankly at me, then to the woman. "I said get the fuck up now!" I am angry, but focused. I am waiting for the man to produce a knife. I will have to shoot him.

My yelling has drawn other searching officers in a jog toward my location. The man breaks his glance and looks toward the approaching group. He rises slowly and the woman slinks to the ground, crying. "Get your hands on the hood of my car, now!"

The man complies and is handcuffed by another officer, as I cover him with my handgun, ready to shoot if necessary. The shot never comes. He is taken into custody without a fight. Apparently, his toughness only surfaces when his opponent has no means of defense. Moments later, a gun is found in the weeds mere feet from where I first encountered the man and woman.

When I go to the woman, she is hysterical. She cries and clings to my uniform, pulling me down into the grass. We sit for a moment as I try to calm her. Other officers deal with the suspect as sirens wail in the distance. When we finally get up the woman stops quickly and vomits on my boots.

"He was going to kill me," the woman sobs, as she grabs my arm tighter.

"You're okay now. He's not going to hurt you," I tell her as we trudge onward.

In the back seat of a patrol car, the man stares at us out the window. I shield her from his glare as we walk past and meet two paramedics. The woman defiantly refuses a stretcher until she nearly collapses about 25 feet from the ambulance. It is, I think to myself, her way of proclaiming she is a survivor.

I don't think anybody here would question that fact.

As the woman and her family, who had also been part of the ordeal, head to the hospital, the suspect is taken to jail. My hope is that his last moments as a free man have expired.

Mercifully, the rest of the night passes quietly. As I reflect upon my shift and the places it has taken me, I think of the irony that a good day for a cop usually necessitates that it was a bad day for somebody else. It's during the heat of battle - during the times when we're put to the test - when cops are able to reassure themselves that they're here for a reason. I guess that's just the way it works.

Today I feel like I have a purpose. Today I very well may have saved a life. Today was a good day.

I wish every day were this good.

Ride-A-Long

A basketball sits motionless in the early summer grass. Just a few feet away a young boy lays equally still as a cop and two paramedics try in vein to coax life back into his limp body. It is late afternoon on a gorgeously sunny day in early June as I help string crime scene tape around the area where the boy was shot. I ask as politely as possible for bystanders – several dozen people from the neighborhood have gathered to watch this young man die - to move back from the scene.

"Sarge, I'll follow the rig to the hospital," I advise a supervisor at scene. When the boy officially expires his body will become evidence and it will have to be escorted by an officer until it reaches the morgue. "Okay East, let me know," the supervisor responds. "Let me know" in this instance is code for "tell me when *a doctor* says he's dead."

A few feet from my patrol car I turn and see Jim wandering in the street near the ambulance. I had almost forgotten he was here. His face is slightly ashen as he looks at me with eyes that seem a thousand miles away. "That isn't good," he says quietly, sadly. I try to force a sad expression for a moment. "No. No it's not," I reply softly. Jim looks like he wants to vomit. I'm not really sure why, but it is not quite the reaction I had expected.

We had arrived here about 15 minutes ago at the end of a nerve-racking, warp-speed drive from Saginaw's north end. My patrol car shuttered, shook and slid slightly sideways as I made the curve southbound on N. 5th Street through a small tunnel which runs underneath a rail yard, a line of train cars sitting 20 feet above while I struggled to keep my tires firmly on pavement. My accelerator was pressed hard to the floor and controlling my Chevy Impala required nearly all of my attention. Still, I glanced from time to time at Jim as he sat to my right, gripping the interior door handle.

It was a couple weeks ago that I invited Jim, the father of my son's best friend, to come on a ride-a-long with me at work. We had talked often recently while watching our sons play for a local high school baseball team, and I immediately sensed Jim's interest in police work. Despite running an obviously successful company of his own, Jim, like many people I meet, seemed to have a curiosity about police work. I wasn't surprised when he took me up on the offer to accompany me for a shift.

Jim had shifted slightly in his seat moments ago as we rocket down N. 5th Street passing the green-and-white signs which mark the cross streets - Wadsworth, Tuscola, Johnson, Lapeer, Federal. Within seconds we were approaching Janes Street, where I braked only long enough at a red light to ensure my path was clear. My patrol car siren blared loudly and radio chatter filled the car as Jim looked over his shoulder to gauge the distance of another patrol car, its top lights also ablaze, which was following in our path.

A few moments prior, the officer driving the second patrol car had accompanied us as we checked out a possible stolen vehicle on the far north end of town. Ironically, Jim and this officer had both attended high school locally and knew a lot of the same people. They chatted comfortably and I sensed their connection made Jim more at ease spending the day in a cop car.

"Man, this is your first ride-a-long – we've got to get you to a shooting or a homicide or something," the officer had joked prophetically to Jim moments ago. It was the type of absent-minded comment cops frequently make. Ride-a-longs so often turn out to be a let down for action-seeking civilians. Commonly, somebody will sign up for a ride-along, expecting to see the death, mayhem and violence they hear cops ramble on about at parties or family gatherings, only to show up and suffer through the only boring day of the month.

I came to the conclusion long ago that taking a ride-a-long is a double-edged sword. While I often beg for the calm of a quiet day on the streets – I have seen enough death – I know a person riding in a cop car for the first time wants to experience much more than a Sunday drive. So it is when I have a civilian partner, I find myself praying for just enough action to keep them awake. Staying awake this day would not be a problem for Jim.

Our drive to the hospital is quiet. I think this is the first time Jim has seen somebody killed and he is still processing the sights, sounds and smells. "Anyway, our job now is to wait with the body until they pronounce him," I tell Jim. "Then we'll have to follow the body to the morgue and write a supplemental report for the case file, stating what we did." Jim stares at me blankly for a moment then responds with a flat "Okay."

The scene at the hospital emergency room is pure chaos. There are 15 or 20 people in the room with the young boy as soon as he is wheeled in. There are aides and nurses and doctors and surgeons. And there is blood, an unbelievable amount of blood. I stay outside the room, but peer in to watch the goings on. People rush in and out carrying various tools of their trades as they try desperately to save this young man's life.

Jim follows me outside when I go to my patrol car to call the shift commander and update him on the situation. "No, they're still working on him, but it doesn't look good. I'll get back with you back when they call it, probably won't be more than 15 minutes." When I hang up the phone, Jim is standing on the other side of the patrol car. He is staring across the street at a park, but I am sure he does not see it.

"You, um, coming back in?" I ask.

"No. I . . . I think I'll stay out here for a bit," Jim replies.

As I punch in the access code to open the employees-only emergency room door, I look back briefly at Jim. He is on his cellular phone. His son is not much older than the boy who is now dying inside this hospital, and his daughter is the exact same age. He probably saw them only hours ago, but I think he misses them both very much right now. I am sure he is calling home.

It takes longer than expected, but eventually a doctor approaches me. "He's gone. One gunshot about here," the doctor says. He demonstrates by fingering a spot on my lower back near the bottom of my bullet-proof vest. "It ricocheted up and went right through his heart."

This information neither saddens nor sickens me. I've been through this routine dozens of times before. Numbness, I suppose, is a hazard of being a cop. "Thanks, doc," is my only response.

When I turn, Jim is standing next to me again. He had come back inside just in time to hear the news. He looks, deep down, like he wants to cry, but I know he doesn't want to do it here. This is the macho world of police work, and I sense Jim feels a little vulnerable right now. Real men don't cry, right? Nothing could be farther from the truth.

"I'm gonna go back outside for a bit," he says.

"Okay. Come back in whenever you're ready."

An hour later, Jim and I follow two hospital staff members as they wheel the sheet-covered victim to the morgue. They walk fast and we struggle to keep pace. "We don't want anybody to see him," one of the attendants says, explaining that a good customer relation – hospital visitors should not see dead bodies – is the reason for our brisk pace. Moments later we arrive at the morgue, an unassuming, refrigerated room located in a lower-level back hallway. It takes 20 minutes or so and a lot of re-arranging before they can find room for the deceased boy. A lot of people dying lately, one attendant matter-of-factly explains.

Another minor shooting is dispatched as Jim and I head to the police station where I need to tag evidence and write a brief report. The streets are getting busy, I explain, so

I'm sure there will be plenty more action tonight. Jim responds with a slight smile. He appears to be shaking off the effects of the dead boy.

We run some calls for service as darkness settles over the city, but they are not of an unusual nature. An hour or two after dark, we continue our patrol as I show Jim the sights of my assigned district.

"This is one of the hotter drug areas," I tell Jim as we pass through 4th and Kirk. This neighborhood is named for the two streets which mark the intersection at the epicenter of this especially violent nook in Saginaw's north end. I explain the history of the area and how the heroin craze of the 70s, I was told, was replaced by crack cocaine in the 80s. Crack continues to drive the drug trade even today. Jim listens attentively and seems interested as we pass a house where eight or ten people mill about in the front yard. "That's a lot of people hanging out this late," I say aloud to no one in particular as we roll slowly past.

Less than two minutes later we are pushing south on N. 5th Street near Lapeer when a dispatcher breaks the radio's calm with details of another shooting. The location is the house we passed moments ago. "We just left there," I mutter, shaking my head. Jim looks at me slightly confused and is not sure what to say as I bring our car's tired lights and siren to life again and inform Central Dispatch we'll be responding to the shooting from a few blocks away.

Our arrival at the scene takes less than a minute, and we're enveloped in sheer mayhem. When my patrol car makes the corner 100 feet away, the quiet gathering of people we had seen just moments before is now a screaming mass, yelling for help. As I run for the porch where several people are pointing to a victim, I simultaneously ask central dispatch for an E.T.A. on the ambulance. Without even seeing the first victim, instincts tell me the hysteria gripping this house is an indication of the seriousness of his wounds.

Beside the front porch a man lays gushing blood from a wound which appears to be near his lower abdomen. Another man is pressing a towel on the hole. "Keep pressure on that; keep doing what you're doing," I tell him. Still there are no ambulance sirens. "Central, how far off is the rig?" I yell into my portable radio, wondering why this question wasn't answered the first time. *Maybe the dispatcher did answer and I just didn't hear.* I look and see Jim now standing on the front lawn as people run up and yell to him. "Can anybody tell me who did the shooting?" I ask. Various vehicle descriptions are shouted out. Sirens yelp now in the distance, but I can tell they are police cars, not ambulances.

"Hey, the other one's inside!" someone yells at me.

"The other who?"

"The other guy that got shot; he's in there."

I make my way inside the house, tracking bloody footprints behind me and find another man soaked in crimson. His wounds appear less severe than the man outside, but they are not minor. "Central, how far is the rig?" Several patrol cars scream up the road and the roar of their engines offers the slightest bit of relief. I've been here less than a minute, but my mind is overwhelmed and can barely separate and process all the words, thoughts, sights, sounds and smells being hurled at me. More officers at the scene will at least dilute the information being directed my way.

As I deal with the man inside the house, I yell out the door at the next responding officer that the man beside the porch is the most severe. Through a haze of people and red-and-blue overhead lights I see Jim in the front yard, but my mind pauses on him only for a moment as an ambulance finally arrives.

The man applying pressure to the guy near the porch refuses to let the paramedics near his friend. Adrenaline has taken over and the man simply cannot think straight. An officer backs him off the wounded man with the threat of a taser, as the people in the yard look on in shock. The tactic might seem extreme, but the victim lying near the porch appears on the verge of bleeding out, and he needs help now.

Another ambulance arrives. There are also eight or 10 cops on scene now, as the crowd has grown somewhat hostile. I retreat from the house, leaving the second wounded man in the care of medical staff. Outside, I gather what few witness statements are being offered and then retreat to the outer perimeter of the scene to assist with stringing crime scene tape and pressing back the multiplying number of onlookers.

Some people have rushed the ambulance where the more severe of the victims is being treated. A few leave when told, others have to be physically removed. I open the ambulance door and ask an officer inside if he needs help. "Man, I'm dying," the victim mutters. "Just keep those people away from the rig," the officer says, never breaking his gaze from the victim and the paramedics struggling to save his life.

A few moments later, we breach the police tape to let the ambulance out and then re-secure the scene. A drunken woman screams incoherent obscenities at me, but skitters away when I approach her to see what she is babbling about. She returns to the perimeter when I walk back to the center of the scene.

Near my patrol car Jim is standing silently, taking it all in. The injured have been whisked away now. The families and friends have also departed for the hospital. Witnesses have been secured. The scene is eerily quiet. A few dozen faces stare silently from the darkness beyond the yellow tape. A supervisor and the few remaining officers stand nearby, talking over the events of the past 15 minutes.

Jim quietly listens as I walk over and make small talk. Mostly I joke about what a crazy day it's been and how he has seen more than most ride-a-longs get to experience. He responds and even manages a smile or two, but there is an air of uneasiness about him now that he just cannot shake.

"When you were inside people kept running up and yelling things to me," he finally says. "Why would they do that?"

"Well, you're a white guy in an all black neighborhood. You showed up in a cop car, so they probably thought you were a cop," I tell him.

Over the next few minutes I make sure to introduce Jim to the few officers that remain at scene. It seems the polite thing to do. We small talk back and forth, but what we're really doing is killing time until the inevitable happens. Finally the radio call comes. The first victim, the man lying near the porch when we arrived, has died. He muttered moments ago in the back of the ambulance that he was dying. Those words have now become fact.

Jim appears startled to hear the news. He stands silently as the supervisor at scene lays out a game plan. She needs to divide up our already strained manpower. The scene will be held now for detectives and possibly the state police crime lab. Then the police radio bellows word of another shooting on the southeast side of town. Two officers break from the scene to head to the next tragedy.

Half an hour or so later, I am relieved by another officer from guarding the homicide scene. As we make the two-mile drive back to the police station where I will string up bloody clothing to dry in an evidence room and string together words to describe the bloodshed, I sense Jim has a thousand questions. Most of them, I am sure, begin with "why?" The questions never come, and this is a good thing for I have no answers. Even after 15 years.

It's is around 1 a.m. and the shift is still two hours from ending. My next hour or so, however, will be consumed with documentation. I tell Jim he won't be missing much if he leaves a little early and he quickly agrees. When we part with a handshake, there are a million words that need to be spoken, but none are given voice. He simply cannot make sense of the day's experiences. I have gave up trying years ago. Jim drives off silently into the night, a vastly different person, I think, than he was just 10 hours ago.

As I finish my report I ponder Jim's reaction – sadness, pain, compassion and confusion - to the day's events. And it occurs to me that despite the tragedy of this day, I felt none of these things, at least not enough to recognize. A 12-year-old boy died right in front of my eyes and my heart barely skipped a beat. The numbness has all but consumed me now and the deep well of compassion I possessed prior to becoming a cop has nearly run dry.

I am stirred from these thoughts as Central Dispatch puts out another call for another human tragedy in another part of town. I clear and volunteer to take the call. My night extends until nearly 5 a.m. as the officers on my shift are ordered to work overtime in an attempt to get the streets under control. The birds are chirping at full volume by the time I make my way home.

Several days later as I muddle through some mundane household chores, the telephone rings. When I answer, I am surprised to hear the voice on the other end.

"Hey, Mike?"

"Yeah?"

"This is Jim. Listen, I just wondered . . . did they ever catch the person who shot that kid?"

The question catches me off-guard and I pause for a moment. There have been many others shot, stabbed and beaten since that night, and I have to send my brain into a quick rewind before I can process the question Jim is asking. Suddenly I picture a boy. He is lying motionless in the lush green early summer grass near a basketball that will soon have no owner.

I had forgotten all about him.

How sad.

Author's Note: As of this writing neither the killer of the 12-year-old boy nor the killer of the man shot later in the evening have been identified. Jim has not accompanied me again on a ride-a-long since this night.

The Drive

The 70 or so miles of Interstate 69 between Flint and Port Huron is a brutally dull stretch of road, but the budding trees of early spring help soften the edges of boredom. I am alone on a trip back to my hometown to spend a few hours with my mother. It is a trip I know I should make more often.

The radio offerings are limited – I won't be able to pick up *89X* out of Windsor, Ontario, for another 20 miles – and my mind wanders like it always does on these trips. As usual, I think a lot about my job, my family, where I have been and where I am going.

I used to travel this route going back and forth to college years ago. The four-hour trip to and from Ferris State University was always filled with anticipation. The excitement of coming home on break a more mature person than when I left was matched only by the anticipation of returning to school to continue experiencing the freedoms that only college life can offer. I often long for my college years when life, much like daily classes, could simply be blown off for days at a time without concern for the consequences. Things have grown much more complicated since then.

My father's fight with brain cancer is over now. Some days were better than others, but each passing day brought horrors slightly worse than the day before. The struggles I have faced in 15 years on the streets pale in comparison to the pain, anger and confusion he faced every hour of his final years.

163

The past strains of our relationship had long since melted away when he died; the reality of death has a way of making such things seem petty. Through the years my father managed to instill in me the values of hard work, integrity and humility that serve me well as a police officer. You can't ask much more of a father.

Pushing her mid-60s now, my mother has also found peace in a life that has been ripe with challenges. She found permanent sobriety on a single day some 25 years ago. She enrolled in college, earned a degree and now holds a supervisory position at a hospital near her home, where she is often called upon to work overtime when others prove undependable. Her vices now consist of an occasional trip to the casino and spoiling her grandchildren. After two unsuccessful marriages, she swore off men years ago. "What do I need a man in my life for? I am perfectly happy with just me." she once proclaimed. My mother is at peace. It is the elusive type of total contentment I hope to find someday.

Half an hour later I am exiting the expressway on the fringes of Port Huron's north end, but my mind still wanders. I think about my career, and about the violence, hatred and death I've seen. I think about the murdered teen from yesterday's shift and the grief and outrage of his family and friends. If only someone had cared that much when he started running with a street gang, maybe the bullets never would have found him. I remember his face, at least for today, but I can't remember his name. *What was his name?*

My mind takes mental pause as I pass a baseball diamond where my friends and I played pick-up ball when I was a teen. I was always an average ball player at best, but my days on this field provided a much-needed distraction in my life. These happier memories bring a smile to my face.

A few blocks later I pass a boarded-up family market where I used to buy *Twinkies* for 13 cents a pack when I was a kid. The store closed decades ago, falling, like most other mom-and-pop markets, to the neon-lit, 24-hour convenience stores where I now often respond to armed robberies. I used to find refuge from my own problems inside this store, if only for 10 minutes at a time. If this place was still open I would stop in right now.

Compared to my friends my upbringing was extraordinary, to say the least. But sometimes now I think that God might just have planned it that way. Maybe all of the trials, heartaches and outright suffering of my youth were simply to prepare me for what was ahead – becoming a cop. Maybe He prepared my past to prepare me for my future. I don't know if I would have survived the job this long had I not had personal experience with many of the problems with which I now try to assist others.

I arrive at my mother's house earlier than expected. The door is locked and the driveway is empty. It's not unusual for my mom to be held over at work on any given day, and she hasn't gotten home yet.

When I unlock the door and go inside, I immediately grab a handful of candies, like I always do, from a glass dish on top of the television. I walk around, absent-mindedly inspecting the home where I grew up while briefly re-playing in my head bits and pieces of my childhood. The living room color scheme has been changed a few times, and the kitchen was re-done years ago. In my old bedroom a few painted-over dents are still visible in the plaster on one wall.

I am startled back to reality by the sound of the garage door opening. My mom is home from work. When she walks in the back door, she is as upbeat as ever, and she greets me with the same cheerful smile that she always seems to have. It's a smile I seldom saw as a child. "Hello, Michael," she says.

At least she didn't call me Mick.

Final Thoughts

This journey began for me far more than a decade ago. Many days it seems it will never end.

I was just 29 when I accepted the offer to become a police officer in Saginaw, Michigan, as challenging a town as any to work as a cop. On that day my law enforcement career began and I pulled away from the platform on a journey which has carried me to many places I never knew existed, neither in society, nor in my own mind.

The journey of my cop career has been a wild ride, and there are days I long for an end to the senselessness, death and violence; an end to *The Fight*. There are some days I want to break down and cry and other days that I want to beat the living hell out of those who bring so much pain upon others. Most often I give voice to neither my sorrows nor my anger. It's easier to just file away those emotions and deal with them later, if at all.

Over the years *The Fight* has become tiring, and it wears on me daily. There are ways to get free – to escape the profession I strived for so many years to become a part of. But I will not give up *The Fight*. Not yet.

The carcasses of the officers I have known – those who have stood beside me to combat sheer evil - litter the path of my journey.

Many former officers have reached the brass ring of retirement, some of them fading away quickly, the way a vivid dream melts from the subconscious at first awakening.

Fed up with the madness, they disappear never to be seen nor heard from again.

Others show up at the police department from time to time, looking older than their years, re-telling cop stories and joking about how nice it is to be away from it all. But there is a tangible sadness in each of their faces. The spark in their eyes, and the fight in their souls, is gone. Through their jokes I can see they would give anything to feel the rush of a cop's life just one more day. But those days are gone. What they have left to sustain them is a regular pension check, a lifetime of memories and an odd hollowness in their hearts.

Other cops walked away suddenly; walked away from their uniform, their badge and their career, the promise they gave to "Serve and Protect" eventually becoming more than they could fulfill. They work now in a variety of other run-of-the-mill jobs, jobs I cannot picture myself working just yet. I will not walk away from *The Fight*.

A few former co-workers landed in jail or prison as they ultimately allied themselves with that which they had vowed to oppose. They used to be my backup, and I once relied upon them to keep me safe. I will not sell out to *The Fight*.

Two other co-workers left in more tragic ways. One walked away from Saginaw mid-career, swapping the violence of urban police work for the promised calm of rural law enforcement. His demise came at the end of a rope tied by his own hands. The other departed on a mental health disability, claiming the constant up-close contact with death had left her disabled. Some officers joked that she had found the perfect early retirement deal . . . until she shot herself in the head one day. They don't joke about her anymore; neither do I. But I pray for them both from time to time. There was no public outcry for the lives of these two and what the premature demise of each represents. *Just be strong*, seems to be the public sentiment toward cops. *We don't want to know about the times when you can't be.* God willing, I will not end *The Fight* this way.

Day after day I confront the worst society has to offer, but my destination seems no closer. I can literally see and feel my cop beginnings falling farther and farther behind; I am years and uncountable heartaches from where I began. The physical assaults, the car chases, the bodies and the tears pile up like meaningless statistics from a long-since-played baseball season. Yet retirement never seems to draw closer, flickering like a mirage in the desert, always there but never quite close enough to touch.

Most days I long to be away from the madness which permeates the streets where I have logged more than 25,000 hours on patrol. I can't help yearning for an end: an end to the violence, an end to the insanity, an end to the hatred which crushes down on me from the streets. It is the same hatred which claws at my insides, wishing to unleash itself upon the monsters I confront day after day. But I cannot let this hatred loose. *The Fight* has its own rules, and they are rules I must obey.

I eagerly await the day when I can watch the late night news and not know the truth. I want to see the breaking story about the man shot dead outside a party store, and not know that he is far from the "great dude" that family members are crying about on the live-at-the-scene video feed.

I don't want to recall the family of a murdered 15-year-old running up to a crime scene, screaming "the po-lice don't do nothing,'" while neither a thought nor a word is directed at the suspect who pulled the trigger.

I don't want to know that the kid who was yanked from a burning vehicle after being shot in the head with a high-powered rifle – his brain matter had stained my uniform sleeve – had a handgun at his own feet when he died.

I long for the day when I can believe that all the innocent victims on the 11 o'clock news might be just that – innocent.

For now, though, I am a cop, and I am saddled with the burden of truth. But I will not give up *The Fight*.

Not yet.

Acknowledgments

A special thanks to my wife, Deanna, who continually preached patience during the process of writing this book, and to my son, Brady, whose kind heart, innocence and enthusiasm motivate me so often. Thank you also to Saginaw Police Chief Gerald Cliff for his support of my writing. Thank you to Lt. Randy Sutton and Professor Peter Moskos for reviewing *Beyond Hope?* and providing not only guidance, but glowing endorsements of as well. Special thanks also to Officer Denny Howe for unmasking his memories of a raw, hurtful event and helping me tell a story which needed to be told, and to Jim McGillis for allowing me to expose a painful story which I am sure is very personal to him. Finally, thank you to Gregory and Linda King, for permitting me to use the cover art that appears on the front of this book, and for allowing me to tell the story of their daughter, Karen, who will forever live in my memory.

A brown worn-out bulletin board hangs at shoulder height just inside the inner door of the men's locker room at the Saginaw Police Department. Pushpins hold in place upon it various programs from the funerals of Michigan police officers. Each work day my eyes are drawn to this board as I pass. I see the faces - Shawn Bandy, Robert Kozminski, Jason Makowski, LaVern Brann and many others – and I have a renewed sense of pride for my job through the price they unselfishly paid. Their stories are as heroic as they are tragic. For all those officers who gave so much, and for their families who will forever share the pain of their sacrifice, I offer my eternal gratitude.

35216520R00102

Made in the USA
Middletown, DE
24 September 2016